Bloomsbury CPD Library: Using Technology in the Classroom

By José Picardo

B L O O M S B U R Y

LONDON · OXFORD · NEW YORK · NEW DELHI · SYDNEY

Bloomsbury Education
An imprint of Bloomsbury Publishing Plc

50 Bedford Square	1385 Broadway
London	New York
WC1B 3DP	NY 10018
UK	USA

www.bloomsbury.com

BLOOMSBURY and the Diana logo are trademarks of Bloomsbury Publishing Plc

First published 2017

A catalogue record for this book is available from the British Library.

Library of Congress Cataloguing-in-Publication data has been applied for.

ISBN: PB: 978-1-4729-4335-4
ePub: 978-1-4729-4337-8
ePDF: 978-1-4729-4336-1

2 4 6 8 10 9 7 5 3 1

Typeset by Integra Software Services Pvt. Ltd.
Printed and bound in the UK by CPI Group (UK) Ltd., Croydon CR0 4YY

This book is produced using paper that is made from wood grown in managed,
sustainable forests. It is natural, renewable and recyclable. The logging and
manufacturing processes conform to the environmental regulations of the
country of origin.

To find out more about our authors and books visit www.bloomsbury.com. Here
you will find extracts, author interviews, details of forthcoming events and the
option to sign up for our newsletters.

Contents

With thanks to all my colleagues and students, without whose support and challenge there would be no experience from which to draw for the writing of this book.

I would like to dedicate this book to my wife Catherine and my two boys Eddie and Pablo, whose patience and understanding have known no limits. Well, almost.

How to use this book

The Bloomsbury CPD Library provides primary and secondary teachers with affordable, comprehensive and accessible 'do-it-yourself' continuing professional development. This book focuses on the effective use of technology to support teaching and learning.

The book is split into two halves: Part 1 **Teach yourself** and Part 2 **Train others**.

Teach yourself

This part of the book includes everything you need to improve your use of technology in the classroom. It is split into four stages:

Stage 1: Assess

In stage 1 we will explore what we already know about how technology can be used to support teaching and learning, reviewing both our experience and a variety of models of technology adoption.

Stage 2: Improve

In stage 2 we will study the key principles and strategies that underpin successful teaching and learning, drawing from research findings and illustrating how technology can be applied in support of these principles and strategies.

Stage 3: Evaluate

This stage will focus on strategies and questions that will contribute to evaluating the impact of technology for learning.

Stage 4: Excel

In stage 4 we will combine teaching and technology by suggesting research-informed ways in which we can use technology in the classroom effectively, supporting and enhancing the processes involved in teaching and learning.

This comprehensive self-teach guide also includes teaching tips, to do lists at the end of each chapter and recommendations for how you can share your ideas and practice with other teachers in your school and beyond. A further reading recommendation or title to discuss in a CPD reading group is also included as well as a useful blog post to read in Blogger's corner.

By the end of part 1 you will have assessed, improved and consolidated your use of technology in the classroom.

Train others

Now that you are an expert in using technology in the classroom it's time to train others in your school! External training can be expensive and in-house training is hugely valuable as it can be made relevant to your training context – the teachers and children in your school. Whether it is a quick 15-minute training session or a series of twilight sessions, there are training plans and advice in this section to help you get started, plan and implement technology training in your school. This section includes:

- advice for running good CPD
- training plans for running quick 15-minute CPD sessions or a series of twilight training sessions.

See page 118 for an overview of the training plans.

Good luck with teaching yourself and training others! Keep us updated on your progress by tweeting using #BloomsCPD.

Part 1

Teach yourself

1

What's it all about?

This book is about using technology effectively to support great teaching and learning. It will look beyond the whizz and bang traditionally associated with the use of technology and will explore practical, pedagogically sound ways in which technology can improve outcomes and add value within a school's context, both in the classroom and beyond. Our focus will be on the great teaching and learning that can happen when technology is used appropriately and successfully, and not on using technology for its own sake.

In the first of this book's two main parts we will assess and investigate what we know – both as individuals and as a profession – about the effective use of technology in schools, and will combine this with research-informed strategies that have been shown to improve the quality of teaching and learning. We will explore well-established theory and its implications on practice, evaluating and bringing together findings from the fields of educational technology and cognitive psychology, among others.

Equipped with knowledge about how technology works best, what makes great teaching and how to make learning stick, we will then develop context-specific strategies to adopt the use of technology when it is pedagogically profitable to do so. The goal will be to integrate technology seamlessly into daily practice so that technology is used almost reflexively, intuitively and without fuss. Throughout this process we will evaluate and reflect on the impact of these strategies, picking out the best and using them as the basis of a school-wide professional development programme with the effective use of technology at its core.

The provision of technology-focused CPD often promotes the use of eye-catching digital tools and equipment without due consideration to pedagogical factors and, crucially, the individual school's context. In the second part of this book we will look more closely at the knowledge and skills required to design, plan and implement an effective, technology-focused CPD programme that will have a positive and lasting impact on practice.

Using technology to support teaching and learning

Technology is nothing more and nothing less than the application of technical knowledge for practical purposes. Technology is helpful; that is why we use it every day: computers, fridges, smartphones, washing machines, public transport, the internet... there is literally no aspect of modern life that does not rely on some kind of technology to function. As we will explore later on in this chapter, when technology is used appropriately, it achieves two main objectives:

- It improves and streamlines processes, facilitating the completion of tasks more effectively and easily.
- It allows us to do things that would be inconceivable without the use of technology.

In the school context, technology enables us to focus on *smart work*, instead of *hard work,* and challenges us to be open to doing things in novel ways, so long as the outcomes justify the application of technology to a particular aspect of teaching and learning. On the other hand, like most things, technology can also be used badly, so that, rather than promote successful teaching and learning, it detracts from it. Professional judgement is, as ever, required.

From this perspective, those wishing to use technology to support the teaching and learning that goes on in their schools and classrooms need a two-pronged approach:

- They need to become familiar with the technology used or proposed to be used in their context.
- They need to possess a deep understanding of what great teaching and learning looks like and how it is achieved.

The task seems daunting, but it is not as difficult as you might first imagine. You do not need to be some sort of superhero teacher, but rather have an interest in what technology can do for teaching and learning while at the same time being an open and reflective practitioner who is able to apply their ever-expanding knowledge and skills as a teacher to the application of technology for practical purposes in the classroom.

The technology that is available across different schools will vary greatly. In some schools, technology will be limited to one or two computer rooms and intermittent access to the internet, while in other schools, technology might pervade every aspect of teaching and learning, with all teachers and pupils having access to a tablet or laptop with reliable internet access. Perhaps your school is somewhere in between. Whatever the case, you need to be prepared to work with what you are given, so developing a realistic appreciation of your context and an honest appraisal of what is achievable within it will need to become your top priority. There is a questionnaire coming up in chapter 2 to help you with this process.

Models for technology use in schools

In order to gain a better understanding of how technology can support teaching and learning, it is probably a good idea to explore conceptual models that explain technology's impact on existing practices, and also how technology can act as a catalyst to help teachers and learners conceive ways to teach and learn that would have been previously impossible. The work of Ruben Puentedura is often called upon to illustrate how technology can be used on a spectrum ranging from substitution to redefinition.

In his SAMR (Substitution, Augmentation, Modification, Redefinition) model, Puentedura establishes a clear distinction between mere enhancement – technology that can be used as a substitute for other tools, perhaps with a degree of augmentation and functional improvement – and transformation – technology that can be used to modify or redefine tasks altogether. The most common interpretation of this model is that the best use of technology stems from its potential to redefine tasks. In other words, using technology to continue doing what we have always done is less desirable than using technology to achieve that which had been previously impossible. Though tinkering around the edges can certainly bring moderate benefits, Puentedura's model suggests that the big educational gains will be achieved when we explore what we can do with technology that we couldn't do before.

The RAT (Replace, Amplify, Transformation) model by Joan Hughes provides a simplified version of the SAMR model: technology can replace other tools, serving as a different means to achieve the same goals; technology can amplify efficiency and productivity; technology can transform by allowing us to teach and learn in ways that were previously inconceivable.

Both these frameworks for technology adoption in schools therefore offer us a useful starting point to help paint a picture to students, teachers and the wider school community that illustrates how technology can contribute to the transformation of teaching and learning practices for the better. However, crucially, these frameworks might also help us understand when not to use technology. Whilst many view these models as a road map for technology integration, others find this interpretation unhelpful because it could be argued that any teacher who uses technology simply to substitute existing practices may not be using technology effectively. In fact, they may be using technology when they ought not to, when other methods are actually more effective.

Perhaps a more illuminating and pragmatic model for the integration of technology is the Technological Pedagogical Content Knowledge framework (www.TPACK.org) proposed by Mishra and Koehler. The model suggests a more complex and sophisticated interplay between the different aspects it suggests make for a great teacher: knowledge of content (what you are teaching), knowledge of pedagogy (how you are teaching) and knowledge of technology (what tools you are using).

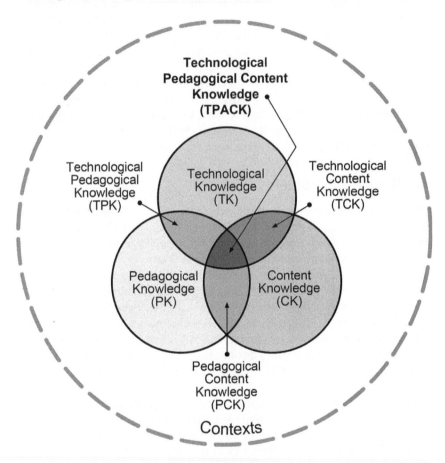

Fig. 1 The Technological Pedagogical Content Knowledge Framework; reproduced by permission of the publisher, © 2012 by tpack.org

According to this model, great teaching and effective use of technological tools are one and the same. As someone with responsibility to provide technology-focused professional development, you will need to think clearly about how technology should be integrated. These models offer a starting point, but please remember that they are not beyond critique. View them as a thought experiment to inform you and help you reflect about what the purpose of technology ought to be in your context and avoid using them as rigid framework that everyone must follow.

Barriers to the adoption of technology

Teachers tend to be very pragmatic folk. They will use whatever works for them, including technology on occasion. Quite probably, you will have noticed that some teachers are more keen on technology than others. Some will jump to be the first to use the latest gadget or web tool with little consideration of the pedagogical benefits while some others will proudly proclaim that they 'don't do technology'.

The good news is that the majority of us don't inhabit these extremes and are somewhere in between. Schools need to have sensible and informed debates about the place of technology in their context, and your school is probably not an exception. It will probably be your job to facilitate this debate, but first you must recognise the obstacles standing in the way of technology integration.

Identifying the problems

1. Fear. When dealing with staunch opponents of technology in the staffroom or the senior leadership team, it's easy to claim that they are afraid of it. But few teachers are actually afraid of technology. In fact, most will happily give it a try if they are given the right encouragement and opportunity. Look around your staffroom and you're just as likely to see teachers using digital technologies to plan and deliver lessons – researching on the internet, putting together an interactive whiteboard flip-chart or preparing a worksheet – as you are to see them wiggling their pens. Some teachers may be more receptive than others, but no one can deny technology is deeply woven into the fabric of our schools and it is here to stay. No one in schools really fears technology. Saying they do turns this into a self-fulfilling prophecy and forces people into unhelpful and counterproductive defensive positions.

2. Support. Teachers rarely have time to learn to use technology more effectively. This can lead to several issues: they are anxious about being made to use technology beyond their comfort zones; and they fear it will not be reliable enough to use in lessons. If teachers aren't supported, they are less likely to use technology effectively. If technology is not used effectively, the value it offers to teaching and learning is diminished. If schools see little value, they are less likely to support teachers to use technology. And that is the conundrum that anyone tasked with providing professional development in this area must crack.

3. Failure. Even when we have all put the effort in, technology sometimes doesn't work. School computer networks are complex environments and the potential for things to go wrong persists. This quietly chips away at teachers' confidence until there is none left and avoidance seems the most practical and common-sensical approach.

These problems have led to the emergence of pockets of vociferous anti-technology cynicism in many staffrooms. In addition to those who think that technology is the solution to every problem, the uncomfortable truth is that there are also many colleagues who honestly believe that forswearing technology results in increased academic rigour and improved outcomes. The challenge for us is to make sure that all colleagues remain open to the notion that using technology *per se* is not the most important factor in this equation, and that it is how technology is used and for what purpose that matters. This way, by studying what currently works and does not work, we can develop a clearer, more realistic, evidence-informed framework for technology adoption. To a large extent, we will have succeeded if we shift the focus of the debate from technology to pedagogy.

Finally, let us take a moment to remember that is certainly not all doom and gloom. In most schools, students are already using technology to support their learning and teachers are already imparting knowledge in effective, creative and engaging ways, supported by technology. Interactive whiteboard flip-charts, word processing, projection facilities and web-based multimedia resources have been features in our classrooms for years. However, let us also remember that the success of a lesson is almost always down to the quality of the teaching, and not the amount of technology that was used in its delivery.

Chapter 1 takeaway

Teaching tip

Whether or not to use technology to support teaching and learning needs to be an informed decision. Consider the following:

- The application of technology should always serve a practical pedagogical purpose.
- Great teachers are experts in subject content, knowledgeable about pedagogy and familiar with the opportunities and challenges presented by technology.
- When it comes to technology, quality trumps quantity.
- Focus on what needs to be learnt, then think about what tools might facilitate the process.

The effective application of technology in the classroom can be very rewarding for both teachers and students, but just increasing the use of technology does not guarantee improved outcomes. Lead by example and show colleagues that you are not an advocate of technology for its own sake, but rather a reflective practitioner who is able to pick the best tool from an ever-growing teaching toolkit – whether it's pens, lined paper, a PowerPoint presentation or an iPad – to ensure successful learning takes place. Wow your colleagues, not with your technical expertise and wizardry, but with how effective your teaching is.

Pass it on

- Be active on social media in a professional capacity – tweet and participate in online discussions and forums about technology integration.
- Start writing a blog that can be both a tool for reflection and a means to define and share your vision about technology integration to a wider public.
- Invite colleagues to regular lunchtime or twilight show-and-tell sessions, with technology and great teaching as the focus. Bring biscuits.

On the one hand it's important to participate in the wider, global debate about technology integration. Don't try to reinvent the wheel. Many battles have been fought by others in similar positions to yours in the past. It's important to learn from their experiences while sharing your own. On the other hand, kick off the debate about what the purpose of technology should be in your own school. Speak to as many colleagues as possible from all areas of the school – heads of departments, heads of year, science teachers, humanities teachers and members of SLT will all have different and valuable perspectives that will help you build a clearer picture about what technology integration means in your context. What are the challenges? And what are the opportunities?

CPD book club

'The Impact of Digital Technology on Learning: A Summary for the Education Endowment Foundation' (see the Bibliography for more details).

Blogger's corner

For an enthusiastic approach to the use of technology in the school context that is firmly grounded on good practice and sound pedagogy, visit and subscribe to Mark Anderson's ICT Evangelist blog: http://ictevangelist.com

TO DO LIST:

- ☐ Reflect about why teachers and students use or avoid technology
- ☐ Write and publish a blog with your reflections
- ☐ Tweet the link to your blog using the hashtag #BloomsCPD
- ☐ Speak to as many colleagues as possible about their aspirations and concerns regarding the use of technology
- ☐ Subscribe to Mark Anderson's ICT Evangelist blog
- ☐ Read the report: 'The Impact of Digital Technology on Learning'

2 Self-assessment

Being able to evaluate your own aspirations and proficiency with regard to the use of technology to support teaching and learning is crucial at this stage in the book. Whether you have an interest in educational technology but have never had the chance to put it into practice or whether you have studied the field to postgraduate level, the shape of any action plan that is derived from the suggestions and advice contained within these pages will be determined by how well you know yourself, how honest you are about your own ability and how thoroughly you are prepared to examine your convictions about what you think technology does and is for.

How to complete the self-assessment questionnaire

On the pages that follow, there is a self-assessment questionnaire to encourage you to start the 'teach yourself' process by thinking very carefully about your current use of technology before you jump into trying to improve it.

When you are reviewing your practice and trying to form a clear view of where you are now and what the next steps will be, there are many ways of approaching it – your approach will depend on you as a person. For some people, it is useful to go with your gut and listen to the first thing that comes into your mind – your instinctual answer. For others, it is a better approach to spend a good amount of time really mulling over the self-assessment questions slowly and in detail.

Quick response approach

If your preference for the self-assessment is to go with your gut only, then simply fill in the quick response section after each question with the first thing that comes into your mind when you ask yourself the question. Do not mull over the question too long; simply read carefully and answer quickly. This approach will give you an overview of your current understanding and practice regarding your use of technology in the classroom and will take relatively little time. Just make sure you are uninterrupted, in a quiet place and able to complete the questionnaire in one sitting with no distractions so that you get focused and honest answers.

Considered response approach

If you choose to take a more reflective and detailed approach, then you can leave the quick response section blank and go straight onto reading the further guidance section under each question. This guidance provides prompt questions and ideas to get you thinking in detail about the question being asked and is designed to open up a wider scope in your answer. It will also enable you to look at your experience and pull examples into your answer to back up your statements. You may want to complete it a few questions at a time and take breaks, or you may be prepared to simply sit and work through the questions all in one sitting to ensure you remain focused. This approach does take longer, but it can lead to a more in-depth understanding of your current practice, and you will gain much more from the process than the quick response alone.

Combined approach

A thorough approach, and one I recommend, would be to use both approaches together regardless of personal preference. There is clear value in both approaches being used together. This would involve you firstly answering the self-assessment quick response questions by briefly noting down your instinctual answers for all questions. The next step would be to return to the start of the self-assessment, read the further guidance and then answer the questions once more, slowly and in detail, forming more of a narrative around each question and pulling in examples from your own experience. Following this you would need to read over both responses and form a comprehensive and honest summary in your mind of your answers and a final view of where you feel you stand right now in your use of technology to support teaching and learning.

- I have done this self-assessment before.
- I only want a surface-level overview of my current understanding and practice.
- I work better when I work at speed.
- I don't have much time.

Quick

- I have never done this self-assessment before.
- I want a deeper understanding of my current understanding and practice.
- I work better when I take my time and really think things over.
- I have some time to do this self-assessment.

Considered

- I have never done this self-assessment before.
- I have done this self-assessment before.
- I want a comprehensive and full understanding of my current understanding and practice and want to compare that to what I thought before taking the self-assessment.
- I have a decent amount of time to dedicate to completing this self-assessment.

Combined

Fig. 2 How should I approach the self-assessment questionnaire?

This is the longest of the three approaches to this questionnaire but will give you a comprehensive and full understanding of your current practice, thoughts and feelings in relation to technology use in schools. You will be surprised at the difference you see between the quick response and the considered response answers to the same questions. It can be very illuminating.

Rate yourself

The final part of the self-assessment is to rate yourself. This section will ask you to rate your confidence and happiness in each area that has been covered in the questionnaire, with a view to working on these areas for improvement throughout the course of the book. The table below shows how the scale works: the higher the number you allocate yourself, the better you feel you are performing in that area.

Rating	Definition
1	Not at all. I don't. None at all. Not happy. Not confident at all.
2	Rarely. Barely. Very little. Very unconfident.
3	Not often at all. Not much. Quite unconfident.
4	Not particularly. Not really. Not a lot. Mildly unconfident.
5	Neutral. Unsure. Don't know. Indifferent.
6	Sometimes. At times. Moderately. A little bit. Mildly confident.
7	Quite often. A fair bit. Some. A little confident.
8	Most of the time. More often than not. Quite a lot. Quite confident.
9	The majority of the time. A lot. Very confident.
10	Completely. Very much so. A huge amount. Extremely happy. Extremely confident.

Fig. 3 Rate yourself definitions

Top tip

Self-assessment is a vital skill for self-reflection and progression in your professional life. It is important that we are honest, kind and constructive when it comes to self-assessing. It can be easy to be too harsh on yourself when you self-assess and allow your insecurities to cloud your judgement. Being objective and honest about yourself and your practice is a hard thing to do and it takes practice. Before you begin self-assessing, it is important to carefully consider the criteria you are using to assess yourself and focus on that at first without thinking about yourself. Feeling comfortable with what you are assessing will lead to a more accurate assessment. If you jump in and self-assess too early, before you have considered the assessment criteria, you may well have a clouded judgement and be unable to learn as much from the process. Don't rush it – it is too important.

Technology in the classroom self-assessment questionnaire

QUESTION 1: How much is technology used in your classroom?

Quick response:

_____

_____

_____

_____

_____

_____

Questions for consideration

- Are there projection facilities in your classroom?
- Is there reliable access to the internet?
- Is there an interactive whiteboard or a visualiser?
- Do you use technology exclusively or are the children allowed to as well?

Considered response:

_____

_____

_____

_____

_____

_____

Rate yourself

QUESTION 1: How frequently is technology used in your classroom?

1   2   3   4   5   6   7   8   9   10

QUESTION 2: How do you feel about the use of technology in your classroom?

Quick response:

_____

_____

_____

_____

_____

_____

Questions for consideration

- Are the technologies and the wider infrastructure reliable or are you forever having to improvise when things don't work?
- Would you say the children learn _more_ or _better_ because of the technology you are using?
- Are the children allowed to use technology? If not, why not?
- Do you use technology exclusively or are the children allowed to use it as well? How often are they allowed?
- Do you feel technology can be more of a hindrance than a help sometimes?

Considered response:

_____

_____

_____

_____

_____

_____

Rate yourself

QUESTION 2: How much impact on improved learning outcomes do you feel can be attributed to the use of technology?

| 1 | 2 | 3 | 4 | 5 | 6 | 7 | 8 | 9 | 10 |

QUESTION 3: What is your general approach to using technology in the classroom?

Quick response:

_____

_____

_____

_____

_____

Questions for consideration

- Do you use technology mainly to project interactive whiteboard flipcharts or PowerPoint presentations?
- Is there a Virtual Learning Environment in operation at your school? Is it underused? If so, why do you think it is?
- Do you use communications technology to deliver feedback?
- When the children use technology, do they do so for research purposes mainly or do they use it to engage in creative tasks?
- Do you feel the children think using technology is fun and engaging? Should that be the purpose of using technology?

Considered response:

_____

_____

_____

_____

_____

_____

Rate yourself

QUESTION 3: How happy are you with how technology is used in your classroom?

1   2   3   4   5   6   7   8   9   10

QUESTION 4: Are you familiar with any educational research, theories or case studies on the use of technology in schools and how has this informed or influenced your practice?

Quick response:

_____

_____

_____

Questions for consideration

- What research or studies about educational technology are you familiar with? What have you learnt from them?
- Do you value educational research into the use of technology in schools?
- Do you consider that you have or are given the time to engage in research? If not, what do you think the main obstacles are?
- Do you feel that researching about the effective use of technology in the classroom should be part of your job or that it should be someone else's job? Have you conducted any research yourself?
- Are research findings discussed by you and your colleagues regularly in the staffroom or during meetings? If so, how valuable are these discussions? What impact on teaching and learning do they have?
- How do you feel teachers and schools in general use or should use research findings on educational technology? What measures should schools take to gauge the effectiveness or otherwise of the use of technology?

Considered response:

_____

_____

_____

Rate yourself

QUESTION 4: How confident are you with your knowledge of educational research into the use of technology in the classroom?

| 1 | 2 | 3 | 4 | 5 | 6 | 7 | 8 | 9 | 10 |

QUESTION 5: How aligned would you say your views and your school's views are when it comes to the use of technology?

Quick response:

_____

_____

_____

_____

Questions for consideration

- How detailed and thorough is your school's ICT policy?
- Does the policy set out a vision for the effective use of technology in the classroom or does it simply contain a list of warnings? Would you describe it as enabling or prescriptive?
- Is the use of ICT seen as separate from your school's wider teaching and learning objectives?
- Do students feel your school's policies are hindering or facilitating? How about the parents?
- How would you modify or improve your school's policies with regard to the use of technology for learning? What would your policy look like?

Considered response:

_____

_____

_____

_____

Rate yourself

QUESTION 5: How closely aligned are your and your school's views on the use of technology in the classroom?

| 1 | 2 | 3 | 4 | 5 | 6 | 7 | 8 | 9 | 10 |

QUESTION 6: Does the department you work in share your views on the use of technology in the classroom?

Quick response:

_____

_____

_____

_____

_____

Questions for consideration

- Do you consider that your department's approach to using technology in the classroom is appropriate and effectively supports the teaching and learning of your subject?
- Who are the best users of technology in your department? What makes their use of technology good?
- Is there reticence or resistance among your colleagues to adopt new practices that involve the use of digital technology? Why do you think this might be?
- Are there clear departmental guidelines on the use of technology in the classroom? If not, what form would they take if it were up to you?

Considered response:

_____

_____

_____

_____

_____

Rate yourself

QUESTION 6: How closely aligned are your and your department's views on the use of technology in the classroom?

1   2   3   4   5   6   7   8   9   10

QUESTION 7: What would you say your strengths are regarding the use of technology in the classroom?

Quick response:

_____

_____

_____

_____

_____

Questions for consideration

- What do you think you do well? What technologies do you favour?
- Have you developed these strengths over time or have you always been a natural user of digital technology?
- Do you find that your strengths have evolved or improved as you develop professionally or have they remained relatively more static? Why do you think this might be?
- Has your use of technology in the classroom ever been praised by students or parents, or by colleagues in formal or informal lesson observations?

Considered response:

_____

_____

_____

_____

_____

_____

Rate yourself

QUESTION 7: How confident are you when it comes to relying on technology in your teaching practice?

| 1 | 2 | 3 | 4 | 5 | 6 | 7 | 8 | 9 | 10 |

QUESTION 8: What would you say your weaknesses are when it comes to using technology in the classroom?

Quick response:

_____

_____

_____

_____

_____

Questions for consideration

- What are you not particularly good at when you use technology? What technologies do you avoid?
- Have you always felt you were weak in this area or has your performance worsened over time? Why might this be?
- Can you think of any weaknesses that you have overcome or improved on with the passing of time? How did this improvement come about?
- Are there any weak elements of your use of technology that have been highlighted by students, parents or colleagues following a lesson observation?
- Has any help or support been available to you or were you left to undertake training or professional development in your own time?

Considered response:

_____

_____

_____

_____

_____

_____

Rate yourself

QUESTION 8: How serious do you think your weaknesses are when it comes to using technology in the classroom?

1	2	3	4	5	6	7	8	9	10

QUESTION 9: Are there any technologies or approaches to the use of technology that you have not already tried?

Quick response:

_____

_____

_____

_____

_____

Questions for consideration

- Have you spotted any gaps or areas for development in your own practice? What approaches have you considered to make these changes?
- Is there any technology or approaches to the use of technology that you would like to try following something you have observed in another classroom or perhaps after reflecting on research you have read about?
- Have there been any obstacles to achieving this? What were they?

Considered response:

_____

_____

_____

_____

_____

Rate yourself

QUESTION 9: How confident are you when it comes to trying something new in relation to using technology?

| 1 | 2 | 3 | 4 | 5 | 6 | 7 | 8 | 9 | 10 |

QUESTION 10: Are there any technologies or approaches to using technology that you have seen work for others but have not worked for you?

Quick response:

_____

_____

_____

_____

Questions for consideration

- Have you ever put a new idea into practice following a lesson observation, a colleague's recommendation, a tweet or a blog you read?
- What motivated you to give it a try? How did it pan out?
- Why do you think it did not work for you although it may have worked for others?
- What role did the different contexts, personalities or subjects play?
- Is it something you would try again? What would you change, if so?

Considered response:

_____

_____

_____

_____

Rate yourself

QUESTION 10: How confident do you feel with your own use of technology when you consider other teachers' practices and successes?

1   2   3   4   5   6   7   8   9   10

QUESTION 11: Would you say that you are being held back from developing the use of technology to support teaching and learning?

Quick response:

_____

_____

_____

_____

Questions for consideration

- What is the main obstacle?
- Are you worried that your weaknesses are greater than your strengths?
- Is there anything that you have tried time and time again and yet you still are unable to make progress?
- Has your line manager helped you identify areas of development and supported you by facilitating training opportunities?
- How long do you spend daily reflecting on how to improve your use of technology in the classroom?
- How did you overcome these hurdles?

Considered response:

_____

_____

_____

_____

Rate yourself

QUESTION 11: How much are these hurdles holding you back when it comes to improving the use of technology to support teaching and learning?

1	2	3	4	5	6	7	8	9	10

QUESTION 12: What would your students think of your use of technology?

Quick response:

_____

_____

_____

_____

Questions for consideration

- Have you ever sought their feedback? What were their comments and suggestions?
- Do they associate technology with entertainment or with serious academic work?
- Do they feel tasks involving the use of digital technology are as important as other, more traditional tasks? How do you overcome this disparity, if it exists?
- Are there high expectations in your classroom when it comes to students' use of technology?
- Have you ever conducted surveys, interviews or questionnaires about how students feel technology supports your teaching and their learning? What were the findings?
- Has your practice evolved or adapted as a direct result of your students' feedback?

Considered response:

_____

_____

_____

_____

Rate yourself

QUESTION 12: How confident are you that you know your students' views and feelings regarding the use of technology in your classroom?

1	2	3	4	5	6	7	8	9	10

QUESTION 13: What do you think students like when it comes to using technology for learning?

Quick response:

_____

_____

_____

_____

_____

Questions for consideration

- What exactly makes children enjoy the use of technology in lessons? Is it when is it used by the teacher to present topics? When multimedia is a part of the lesson? When they are actively using technology for a purpose?
- Are there expectations of how technology should and should not be used? Are these expectations enforced?
- Do they prefer lessons in which the use of technology is a regular feature to those in which it isn't?
- Do students often use technology inappropriately? Do they tend get in trouble when they use technology?
- Should enjoyment or fun be the main objective of using technology in lessons?

Considered response:

_____

_____

_____

_____

_____

Rate yourself

QUESTION 13: How confident are you that you know your students like it when it comes to using technology in school?

1	2	3	4	5	6	7	8	9	10

QUESTION 14: What do you think students need when it comes to using technology for learning?

Quick response:

_____

_____

_____

_____

_____

Questions for consideration

- Is technology something for the teacher to use but not the children? Does allowing the children to use technology result in better or worse learning outcomes?
- Are there strict behaviour expectations? Do you feel they are more difficult to apply or you are more lenient when it comes to children misusing technology?
- Of all the reasons students might give for using technology in school, which are the most effective as demonstrated by improved learning outcomes?
- How would you change your school's behaviour policy and expectations to support the appropriate use of technology for learning?

Considered response:

_____

_____

_____

_____

_____

Rate yourself

QUESTION 14: How confident are you that you know your students' needs when it comes to using technology for learning?

| 1 | 2 | 3 | 4 | 5 | 6 | 7 | 8 | 9 | 10 |

QUESTION 15: What views do you think parents and carers have when it comes to using technology for learning?

Quick response:

_____

_____

_____

_____

_____

Questions for consideration

- Are parents and carers mostly supportive of the school's efforts to harness technology to support teaching and learning?
- Is technology use seen mostly as a threat to children? Why do you think this might be?
- How do children use technology at home? Do parents and carers associate the use of technology with leisure or academic pursuits?
- Do you think parents and carers have a well-developed understanding of the role of technology in schools? How would you improve their understanding?

Considered response:

_____

_____

_____

_____

_____

Rate yourself

QUESTION 15: How well do you think you understand the views of parents and carers when it comes to children using technology?

1	2	3	4	5	6	7	8	9	10

QUESTION 16: What views do you think your colleagues have when it comes to using technology for learning?

Quick response:

_____

_____

_____

_____

_____

Questions for consideration

- Are your colleagues mostly supportive of the school's efforts to harness technology to support teaching and learning? If not, what barriers are there to its adoption?
- Is using technology seen as supporting or opposing traditional academic learning? Is the use of digital technology seen as a gimmick or a valuable tool?
- Is your school's senior leadership team serious about the adoption of technology to support learning or are they half-heartedly seeking to implement recommendations?
- How do you think you could improve your colleagues' understanding of the role of technology to support teaching and learning? Can you see yourself doing this job?

Considered response:

_____

_____

_____

_____

Rate yourself

QUESTION 16: How well do you think you understand the views of your colleagues when it comes to children using technology?

1   2   3   4   5   6   7   8   9   10

QUESTION 17: What would your colleagues say about your own use of technology with students?

Quick response:

_____

_____

_____

_____

_____

Questions for consideration

- Have you invited colleagues to observe your lessons in which you use technology? What has been their response?
- Do you discuss the use of technology regularly with colleagues? Do these discussions take place mostly formally, e.g. in department meetings, or informally, e.g. chatting over a hot drink during morning break?
- Is using technology something that your colleagues understand readily or do you find yourself having to justify and clarify your approach often?
- Have you ever used your colleagues' feedback and comments to reflect on and adapt your approach to using technology in lessons?

Considered response:

_____

_____

_____

_____

_____

Rate yourself

QUESTION 17: How well do you think you know your colleagues' views about your own use of technology in lessons?

| 1 | 2 | 3 | 4 | 5 | 6 | 7 | 8 | 9 | 10 |

The results

Very well done; you have self-evaluated your use of technology to support teaching and learning and you are now a step forward in the right direction to gaining expertise in this area. You have considered your personal approach: whether you enjoy it; whether you feel you have impact; how confident you are in terms of educational research; how well your views fit those of your school and department; your strengths and weaknesses; what you want to try; and your students', parents', carers' and colleagues' thoughts on your use of technology. It is a lot to take in so take the time to let your self-assessment sink in and reflect on it for a while.

Take a look at how you rated your answers for each question in the questionnaire and compare your ratings with the chart below, which will guide you in taking the next steps in the use of technology in the classroom.

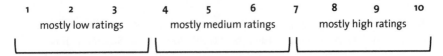

Fig. 4 How did you rate yourself?

Mostly low ratings

You have a way to go with your use of technology, but you are at the start of an exciting journey right now and the sky is the limit. You have a lot to learn but it will all have a positive impact on your students and improve your teaching at the same time. Everyone is a winner. Now is the time to pick your first area of development and really get your teeth into using technology effectively in your classroom. One step at a time, you will develop strategies that will make your job even more satisfying and enjoyable.

Mostly medium ratings

You have trialled a few strategies for using technology in your time and you are most definitely not a novice in this area of teaching and learning. However, there is a lot that you can still do to make sure that the application of technology in your classroom has maximum impact every day with all of your students. You need to take the time to prioritise the areas that you now want to become expert in to take you to the next level. The exciting thing is that you are not that far away from mastery. You just need to focus and hone your skills and knowledge to become great in this area of your profession.

Mostly high ratings

You are confident in your use of technology to support teaching and learning. You have done a lot of reading and research and have a very secure understanding of its potential and its drawbacks. There are areas that you could begin to train others in straight away, to help them master the things you have battled hard to perfect or at the very least make excellent. Identify the areas you can still improve in and make sure you do not get complacent about those areas you feel are already very strong. Always be on the lookout for new ideas that you can learn from others even if you are really confident in your understanding of the use of technology in schools. We can often learn a huge amount by teaching others about something as it opens our eyes to new angles in the topic. Remember professional development never stops.

Now what?

The results are in. So now what? You have a full and detailed self-reflection on your use and understanding of the role of technology in the classroom. It is important that you now make the most of it. Take the time to develop an action plan as a result of the answers you have given and the conclusions you have drawn. Don't make this simply another bit of paperwork you have completed. Use it to really open your eyes as to where you are, where you need to be and how to get there. Prioritise what you want to work on and get started.

Chapter 2 takeaway

Teaching tip

The most vocal views about the potential of technology in the classroom often present as deeply polarised. To some technology is the answer to everything that is wrong with education, whereas to others technology is what is wrong with education. Needless to say, neither view is correct. Most of us sit happily somewhere along this spectrum and understand that technology can be put to good use depending on various factors, such as our context and an individual's ability to use technology effectively.

Bear this in mind when self-reflecting about these answers. Where on this spectrum are you? Where are your colleagues? Are your expectations too high? Or are they too low? Identify what strategies for the use of technology you and your colleagues have seen have impact, and work towards establishing this good practice across your school by sharing it with others.

Pass it on

The start of your self-reflection should be a pivotal moment in your own journey not only towards gaining expertise in this area, but also towards the development of a deeper understanding of the advantages and disadvantages of digital technology within your school and its wider community. What action you decide to take as a direct result of this self-reflection should have a wider impact than just on your own practice. How best to achieve this will depend on who you are as a person. You may prefer to write regularly about your experience and research. Perhaps you favour face-to-face discussions. Maybe your strengths lie in presenting to small groups or leading group discussions. You might even be able to do all of the above. Whatever the case, it is of paramount importance that you find a means to pass on your findings, enthusiasm and growing expertise.

Share and tweet

A brilliant way to share is via Twitter. Cultivate a 'personal learning network' of professionals whose interests you share, and tweet about aspects of your self-reflection that have struck you as interesting or surprising when completing the questionnaire. You may wish to use the hashtag #BloomsCPD to link with related tweets and keep track of the conversation as it evolves.

CPD book club

'Decoding Learning: The proof, promise and potential of digital education' (see the Bibliography for full details).

Blogger's corner

Larry Ferlazzo is an award-winning English teacher, writer and blogger based in the US. His blog is a treasure trove of resources, suggestions and advice, including many references to great uses of technology for learning. His blog, 'Larry Ferlazzo's Websites of the Day', can be found here: http://larryferlazzo.edublogs.org

TO DO LIST:

- ❏ Leave some time after completing your questionnaire and then reread your answers to reflect more deeply about their significance
- ❏ Consider any areas that, as a result of the questionnaire, you now wish to focus on or need to work on
- ❏ Tweet your main reflections and conclusions from the questionnaire using the hashtag #BloomsCPD
- ❏ Discuss the questionnaire questions with your colleagues next time you meet as a department or team
- ❏ Visit and bookmark 'Larry Ferlazzo's Websites of the Day'
- ❏ Read the report 'Decoding Learning: The proof, promise and potential of digital education'

3

Getting to grips with the key principles

As we have already discussed in the previous chapter, the topic of technology in the classroom can elicit a variety of responses and reactions. Traditionally, the debate around its utility has been dominated by bouncy edtech evangelists in one corner, promising technology-fuelled educational transformation. Technology changes everything, they insist. Opposite them stand staunch technology sceptics, reminding us all that, as far as they can see, said transformation is yet to manifest itself after decades of digital technology use. Technology, they suspect, is a waste of time.

The resulting, often acutely polarised debate usually ignores altogether how technology is actually used in our schools to support the daily business of teaching and learning and how teachers and learners continue teaching and learning using whichever tool gets the job done, because, for most of us, technology is neither the problem nor the solution, it is just an option. And so, the more subtle, pragmatic, mundane and almost invisible application of technology that supports teachers and students on a daily basis seems to get lost in the hubbub and is not always taken into account when evaluating the impact of digital technology.

Whilst there is relatively little research that shows unequivocally that greater use of technology will result in improved educational outcomes, which are often measured exclusively using examination results as a proxy, research does suggest that there is a strong correlation between the effective use of technology and improved outcomes. It also suggests that the role of technology in supporting the processes involved in teaching and learning needs to be more clearly identified in order to better understand this role and measure its impact more accurately.

So, what does the research suggest works? Are there any 'best bets' that we can use as a starting point to evaluate and improve our practice? According to the Education Endowment Foundation's Toolkit (EEF) and a report by the Sutton Trust on what makes great teaching, there are key pedagogical principles that research suggests contribute to improved outcomes. Let's explore five of the most important principles and how technology can be applied to, on occasion, help along the way.

Quality of instruction

It may come as no surprise that quality of instruction is key to raising attainment. According to the Sutton Trust report, some of its key findings in this respect are:

As well as a strong understanding of the material being taught, teachers must also understand the ways students think about the content, be able to evaluate the thinking behind students' own methods, and identify students' common misconceptions.

According to this report, effective teachers display strong subject knowledge and deep understanding of how their students might interact with the content they deliver. In schools where technology is used most effectively, teachers understand that pupils' interaction with content can be facilitated and encouraged by technology and that content can be delivered via a variety of media both during and outside lesson time.

How technology can help

Content management platforms (these can take a variety of guises beyond the commercial VLE; we will explore various examples in chapter 5) allow us to create digital learning spaces that complement our physical spaces and support teachers and learners in delivering and accessing content when and where it may be required, exploiting a dimension to teaching and learning that generally remains otherwise unexploited by all but the most technologically adventurous teachers.

Mobile technology may raise more or less well-founded concerns when it comes to issues such as behaviour or the more nebulous and disputable concept of screen time, but it is still perfectly possible to conceive of effective ways in which student access to mobile technologies can support classroom-based or classroom-*originated* learning. Take, for example, what research suggests about testing: it turns out that, perhaps counter-intuitively, frequent testing may be more effective at generating long-term recall than presenting materials to pupils over a period of time and only then testing their knowledge and understanding, as many programmes of study have traditionally encouraged. The implication is that frequent testing may be more effective at helping with the learning than with the assessing, meaning that if students are equipped with or encouraged to use their own mobile devices, the teacher can also use digital testing and quizzing tools to generate frequent and memorable learning events, as well as to assess levels of understanding. Not only does habitual quizzing turn out to be pedagogically sound, but also the resulting automatic data collection can be hugely beneficial to both teachers and learners, who can then exploit it to inform future practice and learning.

Classroom climate and management

Another principle that is essential to foster achievement is classroom climate and management, which covers the following:

> *A teacher's abilities to make efficient use of lesson time, to coordinate classroom resources and space, and to manage students' behaviour with clear rules that are consistently enforced, are all relevant to maximising the learning that can take place.*

Unsurprisingly, it turns out that skilled and effective teaching is key to engendering an environment in which learning and achievement can be maximised. In addition to more traditional classroom management techniques, digital resources can open up a whole new toolkit to help teachers create such an environment. Take for example the fact that curated access to the internet allows pupils access to a wealth of teacher-approved resources. With greater understanding of digital technologies comes a greater appreciation of the need to provide pupils with relevant, appropriate and carefully selected and organised content (just access to the internet in its full but bewildering glory is not good enough) that will remain available to be tapped into whenever required. This may well be during a lesson or indeed outside lesson time – as homework, as extension or for independent study.

How technology can help

In practice, this means that children who finish a task early can continue working using other materials seamlessly. Similarly, children who need extra support with a topic are able to help themselves in the first instance more easily if support materials are always only a couple of taps or clicks away. I have found that interruptions to the flow of the lesson caused by the inevitable *I-don't-get-it* or *I've-finished-what-do-I-do-now* are significantly minimised when appropriate classroom habitudes regarding the use of digital resources are instilled in students.

A single tablet in the hands of a good teacher can also contribute enormously to sustain a scholarly environment during lessons. For example, tablets can be put to excellent use in lessons as portable interactive whiteboard input devices. Wireless projection of the tablet's screen to the front of the classroom frees the teacher from having to be anchored to the board when teaching a lesson. And so, being able to stand anywhere in the classroom when interacting with the whiteboard or projector allows the teacher to spend less time writing at the board with their backs to the pupils, thus providing teachers with new, effective vantage points from which they can react to developments in lessons and, in doing so, contribute positively to sustaining a productive learning climate.

Metacognition and self-regulation

Metacognition and self-regulation strategies have repeatedly been shown to boost attainment, highlighting this approach as one of the most important and impactful interventions to raise achievement. So, what is it and how does it help?

Meta-cognition (sometimes known as 'learning to learn') and self-regulation approaches aim to help learners think about their own learning more explicitly. This is usually by teaching pupils specific strategies to set goals, and monitor and evaluate their own academic development.

The fact that teachers are expected to teach subject content should not come as a surprise to anyone, but comparatively few schools put in place the means and resources to allow their teachers to teach specific strategies that help their students learn, which is surprising, given how strong the evidence for improved outcomes following this kind of intervention is. There seems to be a strong bias in favour of subject content knowledge over pedagogical content knowledge in schools.

How technology can help

Digital resources are often criticised for being a distraction in the classroom. However, this criticism often overlooks the fact that technology can also put in the hands of every learner a set of powerful tools to help them manage their own learning, and that teachers can minimise such distraction by establishing and implementing clear rules and expectations. Indeed, environments where technology is being used effectively are predicated on a culture that views digital technology as a robust scholarly tool, not just a means to access and consume entertainment. Contrary to popular belief, classrooms exist where students don't spend their time playing videogames or sending messages to each other on social media and where technology is used fruitfully and assiduously for academic purposes.

However, it must be said that there are no simple strategies to achieve the levels of independence, understanding, evaluation and ownership of one's own learning that are required for these metacognitive approaches to truly bear fruit. It is down to every school to carefully implement whichever context-dependent strategies they feel can contribute to greater independent learning and self-regulation. The challenges and opportunities that come with the application of technology need to be considered within this wider context. Once again, technology should not be seen as the end, but the means.

Homework

Discussions about homework can quickly become emotive, as both students and teachers can resent the extra work required, usually outside school hours, to complete it and mark it effectively. Let's agree that pointless homework and ineffective, time-consuming marking practices do nothing to support attainment. Instead let's acknowledge that homework can be a targeted, well-designed strategy that can support learning and understanding. Research examined by the EEF suggests that homework can put pupils up to eight months ahead, though they are careful to qualify that it depends on the quality of the homework:

> *There is some evidence that homework is most effective when used as a short and focused intervention (e.g. in the form of a project or specific target connected with a particular element of learning).*

This clearly encourages us to think carefully about what homework we set so that it is effective in supporting learning. Otherwise, what is the point? Teachers in settings where digital resources are employed habitually find that they have a wider repertoire of homework tasks available to them. The fact that students can word-process and research online is often what first comes to mind when we think of technology-aided homework, but the added ability to easily record and edit sound and video, for example, will allow students to produce digital artefacts that help them document their learning and help their teachers assess and evaluate progress in ways that would have been inconceivable without access to these digital resources. But this all depends on the quality of the teaching and the ability of the teacher to set clear, purposeful tasks. No amount of technology will help children learn with homework that was poorly set in the first place.

How technology can help

The concept of flipped learning with easy access to multimedia resources (or, perhaps more accurately, flipped teaching) is one of these new possibilities in the more varied homework repertoire available in a technology-infused environment. Essentially, it involves pupils being introduced to topics or concepts outside the classroom, typically involving access from home to material – often videos – that is produced or curated by the teacher.

In a good lesson, the teacher usually explains a concept or topic, guides initial practice, provides feedback and then allows for independent practice. However, more often than not, this crucial independent practice is relegated to homework, when the teacher is not available to intervene when pupils become stuck. In a flipped lesson – and I am not advocating a permanent flipped state – students have already studied the topic independently and the teacher is on hand to help students apply the newly acquired knowledge to practical tasks, arguably when the teacher's help is most useful. I personally find this approach effective but I can't say it works well with all topics. Professional judgement is, as ever, required.

Feedback

The fifth and final principle featured in this chapter contributes enormously to great teaching and learning and is, of course, feedback:

Feedback redirects or refocuses either the teacher's or the learner's actions to achieve a goal, by aligning effort and activity with an outcome.

Tacit teacher knowledge and understanding about the important role of feedback is confirmed by a solid evidence base. And once again, technology cannot magically make poor or average teaching great, as it is how currently-available technology is used that is the key variable when it comes to formal, school-based teaching and learning.

How technology can help

Having said that, in recent years a wave of digital tools that support the setting of tasks, collection of work and delivery of feedback has swelled. A growing number of schools rely on these tools to support the effective delivery of feedback in various media beyond the usual red pen marking and the establishing of teacher–pupil conversations, generating virtuous circles of knowledge and understanding that inform both teachers and pupils as to how to proceed in their respective roles. Some of these tools are more useful than others and clearly professional judgement is required in discerning the proverbial wheat from the chaff. Always remember, however, that feedback is very impactful but that this impact can be positive or negative. Digital tools can help with the frequency, timeliness and delivery of the feedback, but not the quality – that's up to the teacher!

Pragmatic vs transformational uses of technology

I have deliberately taken a very pragmatic approach in this chapter as to how digital technology can support school-based teaching and learning. However, I am certain that, as the application of digital resources matures, we will begin to use it in ways that have not yet become apparent to many of us. In chapters 4 and 5 we will look at practical strategies and examples of technology used in both pragmatic and transformational ways. For now, I suggest that building confidence among teachers (as well as students and their parents) in technology's ability to support forms of teaching and learning that they recognise is an essential first step before more radical or transformative methods can be formulated.

Chapter 3 takeaway

Teaching tip

Remember that no amount of technology will make mediocre teaching great. Yes, a little whizz and bang might 'engage' your class for a couple of weeks – there is nothing intrinsically wrong with this – but the kind of engagement that will ensure that your class progresses at pace is the intellectual kind. To achieve this, a deeper understanding of successful pedagogical principles is required. Dedicate more time to reading around pedagogy and focus your efforts on learning about what makes great, successful teaching and learning. Only then consider how and what kind of technology can be layered on to support your pedagogical objectives or applied to rethink programmes of study and redefine tasks.

Pass it on

School-based professional development has a tendency to look inwards for 'best practice' to share. I would suggest that you widen the search parameters and begin to look outside your school for such 'best practice'. By doing this, you will be widening the net and increasing the chances of cross-pollination, enriching the gene pool from which great teaching and learning ideas spring.

Consider attending TeachMeets or Show and Tell CPD meetings after school and maybe persuade colleagues from your school to come along. The prospect of a nice drink or a good meal afterwards can be a huge incentive! Perhaps you can organise your own TeachMeet in your school and invite other schools in your group or chain, your teaching alliance or just your neighbouring schools. These events need not be big. The most successful and practically useful twilight events I have participated in were only attended by a few committed and like-minded teachers ready to share and learn from each other.

If your school is not linked to or associated with other schools, then explore what options are available to you. These links do not have to be formal. A Facebook group, a Twitter hashtag or a mailing list can go a long way to becoming an effective and even indispensable source of support.

Share and tweet

By now you have probably gathered that I think Twitter is great for teachers, not because it is in and of itself a wonderful tool for professional development, but because it's a platform for the real tools:

relationships and dialogue. So use the hashtag #BloomsCPD to tweet links to articles related to teaching, learning and technology.

CPD book club

The Education Endowment Foundation: *Teaching and Learning Toolkit* 'What makes great teaching?' The Sutton Trust

Blogger's corner

Tom Sherrington is a former headmaster and blogger based in London. Tom has spent years pondering about great teaching and learning. During this time, he has gathered, among other things, an excellent collection of Pedagogy Postcards. His blog *Teacherhead* can be read here: https://teacherhead.com

To do list:

- ❑ Reflect on the key pedagogical principles covered in this chapter. Consider: how good is my knowledge of the intersection between pedagogy and technology? How can I improve it?
- ❑ Tweet your experiences of applying technology to support these key principles using the hashtag #BloomsCPD
- ❑ Explore ways in which you can link to other schools or organisations
- ❑ Visit and bookmark Tom Sherrington's *Teacherhead* blog
- ❑ Explore the *Teaching and Learning Toolkit* and read 'What makes great teaching?'

4 Overview of the main strategies

Thus far in this book we have explored the reasons why teachers might want to put technology to good use in the classroom and the wider school context, as well as the main principles underpinning great classroom instruction – with and without technology. In this chapter and the next we will begin to look at more practical examples and suggestions informed by both practice and research findings from cognitive psychology, which is the science that studies attention, memory, problem-solving, creativity and thinking. In short: cognitive psychology is the science of learning. So, whereas in the previous chapter we looked at how technology can support great teaching, from now on we will keep in mind the student as well because, after all, the learning and understanding of subject content needs to be done by the student – not the teacher – and because instilling good learning habits in students so that they may exploit technology as a useful aid is valuable.

Like many students nowadays, when I was a student at school I believed that spending hours reading, rereading and underlining important bits before an exam was the best way to learn. But it isn't. It is in fact a very poor way to learn, as none of this does very much for the long-term retention of knowledge and improved understanding that, arguably, are the main objectives of studying. When I think back to when I was at school I can see that I wasn't a terrible student, but I was terrible at studying. Yes, I was good at cramming my head full of facts and concepts at the very last minute that I could recall for tests and exams, but the good grades I often obtained concealed the fact that I wasn't learning very much at all in this way. Every end-of-year exam was an uphill struggle and, as soon as it had finished, I would forget a considerable amount, if not most, of what I had learnt. But in recent years a greater understanding of the principles of cognitive psychology among the teaching profession has generated a renewed interest in what works well and not so well in terms of teaching and learning. So, how can technology support teachers and learners?

In order to answer that question, let's consider briefly what we do know about learning generally, through focusing on how students learn best in the school context. Since some approaches work better than others, it is reasonable to consider what we know about effective instruction and learning to improve how teachers orchestrate teaching and learning. These seven evidence-informed strategies for improving the efficacy of teaching and learning should form the basis of further thinking and research around this area, but I will use them here to highlight how technology could be applied and layered on to support the processes involved in successful teaching and learning.

Strategy 1: Take account of what the learner already knows

Many lessons introduce new topics by referring to learning objectives and then diving into whatever new content needs to be covered. But it would make more sense for the instructor to begin with activities that require students to recall and, in a sense, to activate prior knowledge. This recall approach is supported by cognitive science because it strengthens the connections between existing knowledge and the new concepts about to be learnt. Since research suggests that better learning occurs when students build on prior knowledge, my first suggestion would be to start the lesson with activities that require the retrieval of specific prior knowledge that will help make connections in the students' minds between what's already been learnt and what needs to be learnt. Ditch the learning objectives. They do not contribute to improved learning.

Effective teachers already devise and use starter activities that do just this. This is hardly groundbreaking. And they do this with or without technology. Technology is not necessary, but it can help make the learning experience more effective and fruitful. Think beyond the ubiquitous PowerPoint or interactive whiteboard flipchart. Although they can be useful in the hands of a skilled teacher, they can just as easily be pointless and ineffective. Think instead about how technology can help you achieve something that would have been either impossible or more difficult without it. For example, teachers can use quizzing software to build banks of knowledge-specific quizzes that can be deployed at the beginning of every new topic to link prior knowledge to new knowledge. The effort required to create these quizzes is front-loaded, meaning that once you have created a quiz, it can be reused multiple times without further effort on the teacher's part. How the quizzing is put into practice will depend on your context: are you the only person with access to technology or do your students have access to it too? In chapter 5 we will explore several tools that will allow you to experiment with the notion of retrieval practice supported by digital technology.

Strategy 2: Take advantage of the properties of dual coding

Dual coding is the idea that the combination of verbal association (spoken or written) and visual imagery results in better learning. Well-designed graphic illustrations contribute to depicting models clearly, representing abstract concepts and revealing underlying knowledge structures that help learners make the required connections to enable learning to take place. That's not to say we should populate teaching resources with superfluous illustrations – which in any case often contribute to resources becoming dated prematurely – but that we should focus instead on pairing text with carefully chosen graphics that will support learning by presenting examples and depicting overarching ideas or concepts and explaining how these ideas and concepts connect. In short, we should avoid illustrations that merely 'liven up', 'add colour' or 'add fun' to a resource and use instead diagrams, tables, photographs or drawings that will serve a pedagogical purpose whenever possible. If the answer to the question 'Is this illustration helping students to learn?' is 'no', the chances are it is not needed and you should discard it unless you think it serves another purpose. Many of us prefer teaching resources when they are aesthetically appealing. Although stereotypically we tend to determine academic rigour to be in a negative correlation with the number of illustrations, it is possible to produce resources that are both appealing and supportive of effective instruction. We would be wise not to ignore affective factors that could influence negatively a learner's disposition to learning before it has a chance to occur.

As a teacher, you are probably already capitalising on this dual coding by providing your students with relevant, learning-friendly graphics, tables or diagrams. Great teachers already make the most of the properties of dual-coding in every lesson, using the whiteboard or a PowerPoint to illustrate their verbal explanations. But they might also want their students to create their own. Spending some time during lessons to explain to your students the importance of creating their own diagrams, illustrations and mind maps is time well spent. Not only will they find their own visual imagery very handy when it comes to revision, but it will also help them to organise and conceptualise their knowledge more effectively, so that they remember it more easily.

Both teachers and students can use technology to take advantage of improved learning supported by good graphics. But if you are anything like me when it comes to technology, you have probably found suites of office and design software from providers such as Microsoft or Adobe fiendishly difficult to master beyond the basics. The good news is that these days there is a multitude of web and mobile apps that can help create pedagogically sound conceptual model illustrations with only a few taps of a screen or clicks of a mouse.

Another consideration before we move on to the next strategy is that, using digital resources, graphics can literally come alive. The positive effect of dual coding on learning is also present in video and animations, which can be very useful, though it is important to choose video clips carefully and keep animations simple and purposeful so that they do not become a distraction in themselves. Multimedia graphics and illustrations can then be embedded into digital resources (or linked to from a paper-based resource, using, for example, a QR code) to provide further examples and facilitate conceptual understanding.

Strategy 3: Interleave different but related topics and skills

Interleaving is the practice of alternating different topics and types of content. Although intuitively we feel that we learn better by focusing on one topic or skill at a time, research suggests that better learning is achieved when students interleave different but related topics or skills, rather than focusing on one topic or skill, then another topic or skill, and so on. Although the illusion of better learning is achieved by studying topics in blocks, it is by interleaving topics and skills that long-term retention and greater overall understanding are achieved. This is problematic for many of us, as many teachers and students might find it counter-intuitive when lessons or explanations, instead of focusing on one topic at a time, as is the norm, alternate between related topics and skills as they seek to connect to and build on already existing knowledge. In linear courses (such as IGCSE and the new GCSE and A level), which typically last two years, it is conceivable that a topic that is covered during the first term of the course is never returned to before a hastily arranged revision session just before study leave. Although teachers can claim that the topic has been covered – it would have been – they can't claim to have covered it in a pedagogically sound manner unless they have ensured the topic has been studied more than once during the teaching of the course.

Students and teachers may find interleaving related topics and skills in a programme of study less neat, but the research suggesting interleaving leads to better overall learning in the long term is strong. Once again, good practitioners are mindful, even if only tacitly, that beginning a lesson by recapping what we already know or that which would be useful to that lesson is pedagogically sound, as is setting homework that will prepare students for the challenges of a difficult topic or concept. Many schools already take advantage of the fact that many resources are digital or can be digitised easily, offering teachers the ability to curate them in banks and to create a corpus of knowledge comprised of teacher- or faculty-approved content. From the often overwhelming institutional virtual learning environment to leaner, simpler online platforms such as Edmodo or Showbie, teachers and schools have found ways to let technology help them to manage tasks and curate content effectively.

This curation, like most things, can be done well or badly. Senior leadership in schools would need to allow teachers to spend time and effort applying the principles of interleaving and distributed practice not only to the sequencing of schemes of work, but also to the curation and structuring of digital resources. This can be achieved by structuring the content – with careful hyperlinking, for example – so that students are exposed to key topics and concepts more than once, and by building in review opportunities weeks and even months after new knowledge is acquired, making the revisiting of related topics at spaced intervals become integral to the study of any given subject. The crucial thing to keep in mind is that this can be achieved both with careful lesson planning and sequencing, and with the careful curation of digital resources. As ever, it should not be either one or the other.

Strategy 4: Model-solved problems

Modelling is a very effective classroom strategy, as it ensures that students become familiar with both the mechanics of problem-solving and the underlying principles required to master the topic in question. The student can then be guided to more complex but related problems or questions and, as the student becomes more proficient, the teacher can begin to increase the number of problems or questions for the student to solve or answer independently. Great teaching already makes the most of the powerful effect of modelling by alternating problems with written-out solutions, worked examples – i.e. where the steps to achieve the correct solution are laid out – and problems that the student needs to solve independently. This is also a kind of interleaving (see strategy 3).

Whether you use the whiteboard, a PowerPoint, a worksheet, a booklet or a website to achieve this is of less importance than the strategy itself. What matters is the learning. So, when thinking about using technology, as we will see at the end of this chapter, the important question to ask is 'Is the addition of digital technology for this purpose pedagogically sound?' The answer could be a resounding 'yes'. The humble PowerPoint or interactive whiteboards can be used by a skilled teacher to model problems and solutions to greater effect than using a non-digital alternative, but the more exciting improvement in modelling practice comes from devices that make the most of mirroring technology, such as visualisers or tablets. Using this technology, teachers can snap examples of student work and project them instantly to the class via a projector or screen to model good answers and workings or to highlight and disentangle common misconceptions. There is a case study coming up in chapter 5 that will illustrate this kind of modelling using mirroring technology.

Strategy 5: Teach independent study skills to boost metacognition

Although many schools already promote independent learning by, for example, pointing students to additional sources of reading, relevant websites, video clips, films or TV programmes, few actively seek to teach specific metacognitive strategies to help students become better learners in a given subject. The view could easily be taken that, say, a French lesson's purpose is to teach students French, not to teach students how to learn, which is the essence of metacognition in this context. This view would seem entirely justifiable until one considers the important contribution that metacognitive strategies bring to successful learning. For example, research suggests that encouraging learners how to plan, monitor and evaluate their own learning by providing subject-specific strategies and guidance has a great impact on learning. Effective teaching already interleaves activities in which students are asked to identify where a task might go wrong; to lay out the steps required to achieve mastery of a topic; to produce their own worked examples; or to formulate appropriate questions and provide possible answers.

If, as we saw in chapter 1, great teaching and great use of technology are one and the same, then it is reasonable to speculate that great learning would require that students know both the strategies and the tools they can use to help themselves learn better. Yet schools have typically eschewed the promotion of technology use among their students due to concerns that technology will be misused and become a distraction from learning. This is a real concern, but it is one that can be majorly mitigated both by teaching students how to use technology for academic purposes and by having high expectations of them, as we would in any other area of school life. Acknowledging the problem and at the same time shrugging off a potentially workable solution seems to me shortsighted and contrary to what teaching should entail: transmitting knowledge and transferring the skills with which to apply it and continue learning. If children leave school unable to use technology effectively to further their own learning, whose fault is that?

Instead, let's teach students about online bookmarking so that they can curate their own materials; about personal learning networks facilitated by social media so that they can follow topics, discussions and developments in the subjects they study as they happen; and about quizzing applications that they can use to create their own tests and revision resources. Students can use digital resources to plan, monitor and evaluate their own learning just like we can. But they can also misuse them. That's why teaching children how to use the available tools appropriately is as important as instilling in them the correct learning habits so that they can be better equipped to ask themselves where a task might go wrong;

to break down the steps that they think will lead to mastery of a topic; to produce their own worked examples; and to formulate appropriate questions and provide possible answers beyond those already provided by their teachers or textbooks. These metacognitive strategies are effortful but extremely effective in achieving secure knowledge and understanding in any given topic.

Strategy 6: Frequent assessments for better retention

Tests are generally used to determine the extent to which a student has learnt the required material and to inform future teaching. However, tests are not just good at assessing how much you know and, therefore, how much you still need to learn. It turns out that tests may well be more effective at helping with the learning than they are with the assessing. This is because frequent retrieval practice – recalling concepts or meaning – is one of the most effective ways to ensure you commit something to memory more permanently. Tests tend to be quite formal and often come in the form of high-stakes end-of-unit or end-of-module tests and end-of-year exams. But it does not need to be thus. Given the fairly unequivocal nature of the research that suggests that frequent retrieval practice boosts retention, my suggestion would be for teachers to incorporate frequent, relatively informal retrieval practice through low-stakes or no-stakes testing and quizzing, whereby testing and quizzing are a part of the learning process, not just the assessing.

The implications of this for digital resources are enormous. There are many software packages and digital publishing tools that facilitate the inclusion of frequent retrieval practice opportunities. Even if the resources we are using are primarily paper-based, teachers could consider linking to dedicated web pages where learners can self-test and self-determine where they are in their learning and how to improve. As mentioned above, QR codes and URL shortening services are a great way to achieve this. But testing yourself is easier than ever these days, with a multitude of smartphone and tablet apps as well as web tools that allow you to create your own flashcards and quizzes that you can use and reuse as part of your revision routine.

Strategy 7: Feedback as collaboration

Explaining to students where they are, where they need to be and how to get there is at the heart of great teaching and learning. This is the key notion behind effective feedback. However, providing effective feedback can be very challenging and fraught with unintended consequences, as the impact of feedback is great, but it can be positive or negative. To ensure the impact of feedback is positive, it should be accurate and clear, and it should provide specific guidance on how to improve and not just highlight what students got wrong. Though feedback can take many forms, by far the most common way of feeding back comes on the tails of marking student work. However, the problem is that marking policies in schools range from the sensible to the utterly unrealistic. Many teachers understandably detest marking and feeding back, especially when it's done following a policy that everyone knows has little discernible impact on student outcomes.

But digital technologies can be used to decrease marking workload while at the same time improving the timeliness and efficacy of feedback. Small but powerful tweaks to our policies and practice that would allow us to deliver feedback to a whole class rather than to individual pupils have been shown to be as effective or more effective than the much more time-consuming individual 'What-Went-Wells' and 'Even-Better-Ifs' for every student. You would still need to look through your students' work, but instead of feeding back individually, you would be looking for and making a note of common misconceptions. Then, using screen recording technology, the teacher could record herself highlighting what students have been good at, what they need to be better at and how to be better at it. This feedback could be delivered during a lesson without needing to use any technology, but if you do use digital technology to record it – and this would take as long as marking and writing feedback for one exercise book – you can then make it available so that students can access your advice at any point throughout the course.

With office tools such as Google Apps for Education or Microsoft's Office 365, students can share their work with teachers. When both teachers and students can edit the work, the valuable drafting and redrafting process that would otherwise take a few lessons to achieve can now be accomplished much more rapidly. As we have already discussed, some tools, such as Showbie, allow for comments as voice notes. Given that students can also record their own voices in this manner, I can set speaking for homework regularly and, as a native speaker of Spanish, not only can I feedback on content and grammatical accuracy, as were traditionally the only options, but I can also record myself to model accent and correct pronunciation. Giving feedback becomes a kind of collaborative modelling.

A guide to knowing when to apply technology

A recurring theme throughout this book is the notion that teachers ought to exercise their professional judgement to the application of technology. All the strategies covered in this chapter are effective without the use of technology, so it is important that you can reasonably support your decision to use technology on the grounds that it would be pedagogically beneficial. Here are a few questions to help you with this decision:

- Could you achieve the same objective without using digital technology?
- Would using technology add to your workload or would it reduce it in the long term?
- Since learning is effortful, would your students learn x better with or without the technology?
- Can you explain the pedagogical motive behind your choice to use technology?
- When your students use the technology, will their focus be on the tool or the learning?
- Is the technology allowing you to achieve something that would be otherwise impossible or more difficult without it?
- Would your class learn more, less or the same without the use of technology?
- Is technology being used merely as a tool to engage or to pacify your class?
- What are the opportunities (what you can do thanks to your choice to use technology) and what are the costs (what you can't do because you chose to use technology)?
- Is your teaching better or worse as a result of your choice to use technology?

Summary of the strategies

Strategy	Summary	Digital technology
1. Prior knowledge	Start new topics by requiring students to recall and to activate prior knowledge	• Interactive whiteboard and presentation software • Online quizzing tools
2. Dual coding	Combining spoken or written word with visual imagery	• Design suites (e.g. Adobe) • Digital publishing tools
3. Interleaving	Alternating different topics and types of content	• Virtual learning environments • Content management platforms (e.g. Wordpress)
4. Modelling	Modelling problem-solving and the underlying principles required to master a topic	• Visualisers • Screen-recording software • Screen-mirroring software
5. Metacognition	Encouraging learners to plan, monitor and evaluate their own learning	• Online curation tools • Targeted social media use • Learning to use technology for academic purposes
6. Retrieval practice	Frequent low-stakes testing to boost long-term retention	• Online quizzing tools • Flashcards
7. Collaborative feedback	Explaining to students where they are, where they need to be and how to get there	• Virtual learning environments • Collaborative office suites (e.g. Office 365) • Screen-recording software

Chapter 4 takeaway

Teaching tip

The key to using technology effectively is to know when it can be pedagogically valuable. In order to know this, you need to acquire a secure understanding of the principles behind great teaching and learning and of the challenges and opportunities of whatever technology you intend to use. But it is also important that your colleagues and your students are aware of the reasons behind your choices. There is nothing worse than changing your classroom routine for a lesson observation in which you wish to showcase a new tool or technology. Students will be rightly doubtful about your motives and any observer will come away with the impression that the lesson did not quite go to plan, possibly with very good reason. Instead, take time to explain to your students why you are using the tools you are using (is it to help with retrieval practice, modelling, interleaving?). Invite people to assess your progress only once your students are used to the new tools and they understand the pedagogical reasoning behind their use.

Pass it on

Keep any colleague who is interested in what you are doing appraised regularly – perhaps you have a work mailing list or are writing a blog about your findings. Don't worry about the numbers reading about your work to begin with – even if you are writing it just for yourself, writing is a wonderful tool for self-reflection. You will find that colleagues and, if you broadcast your blog via social media, other teachers from around the globe will slowly start to follow your progress and contribute suggestions and advice.

Share and tweet

Share your progress in applying the principles and strategies covered in this chapter on Twitter using the hashtag #BloomsCPD.

CPD book club

Make It Stick: The Science of Successful Learning. See the Bibliography for more details.

Blogger's corner

The Learning Scientists is a blog curated by cognitive psychological scientists and comes complete with extremely useful downloadable resources, videos and, of course, blog posts aimed at helping teachers understand the principles of cognitive psychology so that they can be applied in the classroom. Their blog can be read here: www. learningscientists.org, and you can follow them on Twitter @acethattest.

TO DO LIST:

☐ Try the strategies suggested in this chapter in your classroom to see what works best in your setting

☐ Introduce your students to the strategies and tools that you will be using in advance of using them

☐ Question your choice to use technology so that it is not merely used as a gimmick

☐ Bookmark *The Learning Scientists* blog

☐ Follow @acethattest on Twitter

☐ Tweet your thoughts, findings and links to related material using the hashtag #Blooms CPD

☐ Find out more about cognitive psychology. Reading *Make It Stick: The Science of Successful Learning* is a great start

5 Putting it into practice

In chapter 3 we explored some of the key principles behind great teaching, with an emphasis on the need to not view technology as a separate intervention – something teachers need to stop teaching to do – but rather as an integral part of good teaching practice. In chapter 4, we looked at learning in greater detail and reviewed some key principles from cognitive psychology. In both these chapters we focused on the processes and principles involved in teaching and learning, and we hinted at ways in which technology could be integrated to facilitate them. In this chapter, we will look at five case studies that illustrate how technology can support teaching and learning more specifically.

Clearly, your own context is critical. Whether you or your students only have occasional access to digital resources or whether this access is ubiquitous (after a tablet, bring-your-own-device or Chromebook deployment, for example) will determine how you can interpret and put these case studies and the suggestions they include into practice. It will be worth considering too how digital technology can be used to support teaching and learning *beyond* the classroom. Although teaching face to face is often preferable, it is not always possible. Avoid unhelpful dichotomies: what's preferable and what's possible are both allowed.

Case Study 1 – Curating resources using digital learning spaces

Surbiton High School uses WordPress, a freely available, open-source online content management system, to curate a corpus of subject-specific knowledge and resources so that students can access them both during the school day and remotely, e.g. for revision at home. The content manager presents the content as a website, whose front page (see Figure 5) features icons representing each subject or co-curricular strand that students can select to navigate to the required section of the site. Each section is then subdivided into further components – typically key stages, year groups or topics (see Figure 6). Menus, sidebars and a variety of widgets fulfilling many different functions can be added to facilitate browsing and navigation.

This is not an ordinary website, nor do Surbiton High School teachers refer students to 'the internet' in its boundless but bewildering glory with minimal direction. Instead, the internet is tamed and the deluge of content is funnelled into a curated stream of relevant, bite-sized chunks of knowledge and resources that students can use in lessons or independently, as appropriate. Teachers provide specific links that contain the resources, including multimedia, that students need to learn about a topic or complete a task. Use of the internet in lessons and at home becomes more focused and, therefore, not only more manageable, but also desirable as an effective resource to support learning.

Fig. 5 Front page of Surbiton High School's digital learning spaces

Fig. 6 Design and technology subsection in the digital learning spaces at Surbiton High School

Mr K leads the design and technology department. In recent months Mr K has organised his department's teaching resources in a digital learning space. All years from Year 7 to 13 are covered. The *Blow Moulding* page in the *A Level Product Design* section features, among other things, the key facts that students need to learn, which are illustrated with relevant graphs and depictions, including video, that facilitate conceptualisation and understanding. In addition, the page features self-marking activities at key intervals that help students secure the required knowledge and gauge their own progress. Mr K doesn't use this page instead of teaching students about blow moulding, but rather to support his teaching and his students' learning of the process of blow moulding.

In other subjects' digital learning spaces, we typically find links to PowerPoints, online quizzes (see case study 5), Word or PDF documents that provide students with instant access to the resources needed during or after a lesson – if the teacher designs the lesson with flipped learning or flipped teaching in mind, she might expect students to access the resources before a lesson. In this respect the digital learning spaces as described here fulfil one of the main functions of the traditional virtual learning environment, that of repository of resources, only at no extra cost to the school, as WordPress is free, open-source software that can be downloaded, installed and operated by non-technical staff with only minimal training and support. However, if your school has opted to use a commercial virtual learning environment, there is no reason why it couldn't be used in a similar way to how Surbiton High School uses WordPress.

Key considerations

1. Think about how your students will use the resources. Simply sharing the PowerPoint used in a lesson will be less valuable to their learning than providing them with both the content they need to learn and the means to learn it (e.g. interactive, self-marking activities or quizzes).
2. Remember that resources in a digital learning space can be used to support both teaching and learning. As such you should aim to create resources that can be used in schools but are meaningful outside the context of a lesson.
3. If you were to design webpages with your students in mind, what would they look like and what would they feature?

Featured digital resources

- WordPress is an open-source (free) online content manager. Go to www.wordpress.org to learn more.
- The digital learning spaces of Surbiton High School can be accessed here: www.learn.surbitonhigh.com.
- Video content in the *Blow Moulding* page was embedded from YouTube.

- Self-marking activities in the *Blow Moulding* page were created using H5P, a free interactive content creator available from www.h5p.org.
- There are various purveyors of digital learning spaces (e.g. LearnDash) as well as a whole host of commercial learning management systems or virtual learning environments (e.g. Firefly, Frog...) that you should investigate. Their price range and functionality vary greatly, so careful research for a good fit to your school context is essential.

Case Study 2 – Modelling using visualisers

Mr M is a biology teacher. His teaching is characterised by excellent content knowledge, a high degree of pedagogical expertise, high all-round expectations and his ability to develop fruitful teacher–student relationships. Mr M's students are confident that he has their best interest at heart and that he will move mountains for them; consequently they too are prepared to go the extra mile for him. In a Year 8 lesson I observed recently, Mr M used his school tablet computer as a visualiser to model the dissection of a lamb's heart. This was achieved by using the folding tablet's case to stand and point the tablet's camera towards the tray containing the heart, so that a close-up image of the heart filled the tablet's screen. This image was then mirrored wirelessly to the front of the classroom, so that the students could follow Mr M's dissection and his explanation as it happened. All 24 students (in pairs) were able to model Mr M's dissection on their own lamb's heart to learn about its anatomy.

Miss K (no relation to Mr K) is a colleague of Mr M. She teaches German and her lessons feature an optimal combination of explicit grammar and communicative language teaching – a high proportion of it in the target language. Like Mr M, Miss K cares deeply about the progress her students make and is an experienced, effective teacher. When I observed Miss K teach a Year 10 German class, she used her tablet to mirror the slides she was using on her tablet in support of her explanation to the front of the classroom, as she paced up and down the central corridor formed by the desks in her classroom. She occasionally ventured into one of the rows of desks to clarify questions or to supervise the work individual students were doing in response to her teaching, as it happened. Because she was not tethered to the front of the classroom, she was able to instruct her students from a variety of vantage points in her classroom, contributing a powerful tool to her box of classroom management techniques. Miss K used her stylus to annotate on her tablet and further explain and illustrate the grammar point she was teaching. These annotations were broadcast live to the screen in the front of the classroom. On two occasions, using the camera on her tablet, Miss K photographed the work of individual students from their exercise books and added the photos to her slides, so that she could display the students' work to the whole class. She then asked the class to highlight what was good about what the students had written in German and how what they had written could be improved, as she continued to annotate on the photographs and the class continued to make notes, corrections and improvements to their written work.

Key considerations

1. Note how the technology supported well-established classroom practice and strategies and did not seek to run counter to them, but rather enhance them.
2. For teachers, high on the list of concerns is lack of time. Modelling using visualisers does not require extra planning and learning to use the device does not require a great deal of technical expertise. It is a simple, straightforward process. Indeed, if the learning is improved because of better modelling, it might result in a lighter marking load.
3. Both Mr M and Miss K used a tablet as a visualiser because tablets are available in their context. Where tablet computers are not available, visualising devices can be purchased that would perform most of the functions described above.

Featured digital resources

- Screen mirroring and wireless streaming can be achieved using hardware such as Apple TV (AirPlay) or Chromecast devices, but also more cheaply using software such as AirServer or Reflector 2.
- The app that both Mr M and Miss K used for their explanations and annotations was Explain Everything. It is available for both iPads and Chromebooks.
- There is a variety of suppliers of desktop or table-mounted visualisers. If you are going down this route, you should read online product reviews and I strongly recommend that you contact several possible suppliers and ask them for a demo on site (not a link to an online video), especially if you are considering buying in bulk. Educational technology trade shows, such as BETT, are great places to see a vast selection of these products in action.

Case Study 3 – Feedback using virtual learning environments

Virtual learning environments (or learning management systems) have been around for some years. With the exception of Moodle, which is free and open-source, they are generally commercial enterprises and can be quite costly. In recent years, more lightweight and streamlined systems have been developed that focus less on providing a repository of resources and more on the transactional aspects of setting and handing in work. In this case study we will see how teachers of English use Showbie, one of these new breeds of online classroom managers, to administer the setting and receiving of homework, as well as the subsequent giving of feedback.

Miss P is a young and competent English teacher who has set her class up on Showbie. This means that she can set work for her class or for individual students within it, track their progress, be notified of the completion of the task (if completed within Showbie) and provide feedback for her students in a variety of formats. In a meeting with Miss P, she talked me through a task she had set her Year 11 students. The task was clearly set out on Showbie and it included a short explanation of what needed to be achieved, followed by a set of bullet points outlining the words, phrases and sources that she expected her students to use. As we scrolled down the screen, I noticed a student had sent a message to Miss P asking for clarification, to which Miss P had replied offering a timely resolution to her query. Despite this digital context surrounding the setting of the task and the subsequent teacher–student communication, Miss P required that her students completed their work in their exercise books. Pen and paper were the best tool on this occasion (a common misconception is that when digital resources are available, they are used instead of other, more traditional resources).

After Miss P took in the exercise books, she read through her students' work and left some shorthand comments as per the department marking policy. I saw ticks, double ticks, crosses and abbreviations such as *sp.* (for spelling) but nothing more extensive in terms of feedback. Instead of writing extensive individual pieces of feedback, Miss P had selected two pieces of work that illustrated the most common misconceptions by students and photographed them using the camera on her tablet. Shen then used the app Explain Everything (see case study 2) on her tablet to record her voice as she went through the work, annotating it with her stylus and explaining orally what had they had done well, what they could have done better and how they could have done it better. The resulting four-minute video was posted back to Showbie for the whole class to watch and derive targets for their own improvement, to be written in their exercise books just above the next piece of work. By doing this, Miss P had found a way to reduce her marking load considerably without compromising her effectiveness as a teacher. Her students went on to achieve excellent results at GCSE.

Miss R is a more experienced teacher and is the second in command in Miss P's English department. Like Miss P, Miss R is a very effective teacher with traditional values. Whilst technology has a place in her lessons, it is fair to say that it is not a prominent place, and this is absolutely fine – we should never seek to replace great, traditional teaching with mediocre, technology-rich teaching, for it's the quality of the teaching that counts. However, when it comes to marking and feedback, Miss R has found technology very useful to her and her students. During a conversation with me, Miss R explained how she had set a task on Showbie, though, unlike Miss P, she requested that her Year 12 students handed their work in via Showbie, as PDF documents. As the students started to complete the work, it became instantly available to Miss R on Showbie for marking and feedback. As there are fewer students in a Year 12 class, Miss R decided to leave individual feedback for each student. What is normally a laborious process involving handwriting corrections, making suggestions for improvement and setting relevant targets for individual students becomes a much easier task. She still reads each piece of work and annotates it using commonly agreed rubrics (see reference to the departmental marking policy, above), but the key difference is that instead of spending a few minutes hand-writing feedback for each student, she spends a few seconds recording her feedback using a feature in Showbie called a *voice note* directly on her student's work, which becomes instantly available for the student to listen to, wherever she may be, as soon as Miss R has finished recording it. In a rare win–win situation, Miss R has found that marking this way is less onerous and more conducive to her own personal wellbeing, while her students have found that they prefer to receive feedback this way, as they are able to hear in their teacher's voice helpful cues, such as tone and emphasis, that are mostly absent from cold, hard, red ink.

Key considerations

1. Using technology does not make rubbish, pointless homework tasks great. Whilst the tools that you use to achieve a task are important, most of your time and effort should be spent on devising appropriate tasks that would take your students' learning further. You will find that giving feedback for work that resulted from a well-designed task much easier than trying to make heads or tails of the outcome of poorly planned homework.
2. Think about what format the work can be completed in. This case study features work that was best presented using the written word, but, if digital resources are being used, it is conceivable that other formats (e.g. video or audio recordings) may be more appropriate, depending on the nature of the subject and the task you devise.

3. Your school may already have a virtual learning environment or learning management system that would allow you to feed back in ways similar to those suggested above. Take some time to get to know the technology that is already available to you and your colleagues better before introducing new technology into the mix.

Featured digital resources

- Showbie is an online classroom manager that helps set and track student work and give feedback. It is available as a web app and an iPad (and iPhone) app.
- Alternatives to Showbie, such as Edmodo (which, unlike Showbie, is free), are available, so do take some time to explore and road-test the features of each of these tools before committing your purchase.

Case Study 4 – Collaboration using Office 365 or Google for Education

Both Office 365 from Microsoft and Google for Education are productivity suites that include the word processors, spreadsheets and presentation tools that we are so familiar with. On this occasion, we will focus on Office 365 as it is used by Mr M, who teaches computer science and ICT. During a series of interviews, Mr M explained how he and his students use the features within Office 365 to manage the coursework required to complete the Computing GCSE course. In Mr M's classes, it is a requirement that students use the *share* option to share their coursework documents with their teacher, giving Mr M editing rights to these documents. This means that, after key deadlines have passed, Mr M does not need to chase submissions but simply opens a folder containing all these shared documents to find and check every student's progress. As he has editing rights to the document, he can add suggestions and corrections directly into the body of the course (Mr M chooses a different colour for his contributions, so that they stand out to the student) or by using the comment facility that places a comment on the margin.

In addition to requiring his students to share documents with him, he also shares a folder with them containing key resources, although this time students have view access only, so that they can open the original documents and save a copy if they wish, but they cannot, for example, delete the original files by accident. There is another class folder to which all students have editing rights, so that they can save documents and resources they find and think might be useful to other students. In addition, Mr M reported how, without any prompting from him, students share documents with each other so that they can work on the same task or coursework item when they are not physically together, even simultaneously. Facilitated by the fact that both Google for Education and Office 365 integrate via single sign-on with the school's IT systems (meaning that students can use the same school user name and password) Mr M has started exploring using *forms* (a tool that allows him to create tests and quizzes) to carry out regular tests and assessments. Students' results are recorded against their names, and a spreadsheet and graphs automatically generated, giving Mr M an instant, granular overview of what they know and, crucially, what they don't yet know so well, thus informing his future lesson planning. In case this isn't immediately clear, the fact that the answers are checked and the graphs are generated automatically means that that there is no marking for Mr M!

Key considerations

1. One of the main reasons why Mr M's pupils do well in computing is because the quality of their interactions (e.g. the feedback he gives them) is excellent. This does not depend on the technology so much as it does on Mr M's pedagogical expertise.
2. Research suggests that collaborative practices have a consistently positive impact on outcomes for students, but students need to learn how to collaborate fruitfully. And this won't happen unless you dedicate some time to teach them how.
3. Besides the usual word processors, spreadsheet and presentation tools, both Google for Education and Office 365 have a number of features available (such as *forms*) that are relatively less well-known but could easily become a regular presence in your teaching toolkit. Take some time to explore and test them.

Featured digital technology

- Google for Education and Microsoft's Office 365 are both free at the point of use. Although a licensing fee is required for Office 365, the likelihood is that your school already pays for Microsoft licensing anyway, so this shouldn't be an extra cost.

Case Study 5 – Promoting retrieval practice using quizzing software

Mr S is a French teacher. He is an active and inquisitive person and these adjectives are probably appropriate to describe his teaching style. His deep knowledge of and deep love for the French language become abundantly clear when you observe one of his lessons, which are purposeful, pacey and intellectually captivating. By his own admission, his use of technology had been limited to PowerPoint or interactive whiteboard slideshows and mp3 audio files, with the occasional visit to the computer suite. It was during one of these visits to the computer suite with his class that he began to realise how effective frequent retrieval practice via the regular completion of online interactive activities and quizzes were to the long-term retention of vocabulary in particular, but also to some aspects of grammar, such as verb endings.

Mr S decided to produce his own vocabulary quizzes using a web app called Quizlet. These quizzes would be either embedded in the school's virtual learning environment or shared directly with students via a URL link. Students then access the quizzes either in the computer suite, on their computers at home or on their own mobile devices. Mr S also uses Quizlet's Live facility or another web app called Kahoot to automatically generate whole class quiz competitions from the quizzes he has saved in the past (or from those created and made public by others). Practically, this requires all students to have an input device available to them – this could be a computer in the computer suite, a laptop from the trolley, a tablet or Chromebook if they have one or, school policy permitting, their own smartphones.

Mr S's pupils enjoy using online quizzes, not because it keeps them busy or it is fun, but because they can see that it helps them learn. As this kind of frequent low-stakes testing ensures that vocabulary is readily accessible to students from memory, Mr M has realised that if he plans speaking activities (themselves a kind of retrieval practice that reinforces learning even further) after completing the online quizzes described above, students can construct new sentences and manipulate language with greater ease and confidence. Importantly, they are not simply reciting a string of sounds to which meaning may or may not be attached, but they are using their knowledge to construct new language as they go, as we would naturally in our mother tongue. The language is fresh in their memory, but responses are not *memorised*.

Key considerations

1. High-stakes testing has a bad reputation, sometimes deservedly so. But remember that the point of low-stakes tests is not so much to assess and award but to help students learn. View them more as another classroom activity or homework task to be used judiciously as part of a well-structured lesson. Explain this clearly to your pupils.
2. Don't dismiss learning key facts (vocabulary, dates, key events and their dates) out of hand. It is often claimed that learning facts out of context is pointless, but remember: a) it is impossible for your students to think critically about that which they don't know, and b) it is your job to provide the wider context.

Featured digital technology

- Quizlet (http://quizlet.com) is a web app that allows you to create, share and embed a variety of quizzes and tests. It can easily be used both in the classroom and at home.
- Kahoot (http://getkahoot.com) is a similar tool. It allows you to create classroom quizzes and automatically generates spreadsheets with participants' scores.

Using these case studies to inform your practice

These case studies offer a glimpse into the classrooms of teachers just like the ones in your school, with varying degrees of confidence and expertise in the use of technology to support teaching and learning, who have found they all have something in common: they have found a way in which technology supports their practice. Be it by helping with the delivery of content, improving classroom instruction, facilitating the delivery of timely feedback or contributing to a reduction in workload, technology has been an ally, not an imposition or a hoop to jump through.

Although the school context – its climate and culture; the training the staff receive; the available resources; and even the socio-economic background of its students – plays a big role in determining the success of the application of technology for learning, the key message to take home is that the teachers featured are all ordinary, dedicated teachers, just like you and your colleagues. None were technology evangelists, whizzes or geeks, just teachers who understood that using technology and great teaching are not mutually exclusive, and that when the right tool, clear purpose and pedagogical expertise combine, great outcomes are achieved. With all this in mind, review these case studies carefully to glean what elements can be transferred to your context, what you can learn from them and, of course, what you could do even better.

Chapter 5 takeaway

Teaching tip

When adopting or adapting the strategies and tools outlined in this chapter, you must ensure that they are suitable to be used in your setting. If anything has grabbed you and you can't wait to give that a go, dedicate some time first to learn about it in greater detail and road-test it before it goes anywhere near your students. Enlist a colleague to act as a critical friend and explain to her what you intend to do and why. If you don't take these precautions you run the risk of introducing a tool to your class before you are ready to use it, potentially undermining any future success if they associate the tool with poor learning outcomes.

Pass it on

One of the digital resources I have recommended in this chapter is WordPress. A good way to get to know how to use it or to reflect about whether it may have a potential use in your context could be to use it as your personal blog. If you do, you will become more familiar with both the opportunities it presents and the challenges you might face in a wider implementation across a school. Blogging will put your thoughts and reflections out there and, in combination with other social media platforms, can put you in touch with people who both agree and disagree with your conclusions. By all means avoid those who disagree discourteously, but don't avoid people simply because they disagree with you. Cherish them, in fact, because they will sharpen your thinking.

Share and tweet

Share your experience of using the tools described in this chapter, as well as others that you might have come across, on Twitter using the hashtag #BloomsCPD.

CPD book club

The Daily Papert (available at www.dailypapert.com) is a compendium of articles, speeches and presentations by Seymor Papert, a mathematician, computer scientist and educator who, through his work combining computing, pedagogy and cognitive science, has made an enormous contribution to educational technology.

Blogger's corner

My own blog, *Shooting Azimuths*, where I reflect about technology and its potential to support teaching and learning, can be accessed here: www.josepicardo.com

To do list:

❏ Get to know the tools described in this chapter and begin to consider their potential application in your context

❏ Share your thoughts and experiences of using these tools with colleagues who can give you friendly and honest advice about their efficacy and how to improve

❏ Blog or tweet about your journey in understanding what technology is good for and what it isn't so good for

❏ Read some of the content available on *The Daily Papert*

❏ Visit my blog *Shooting Azimuths*

6

Self-evaluation and reflection

As you review and implement the strategies and case studies proposed in previous chapters, it's important to pause and take stock. How are things going? What is working well? What isn't? Are any course corrections needed? How can you tweak your approach? Before you continue reading this chapter, stop for a moment to consider and reflect on where you are, where you want to be and how to get there.

Welcome back. The questionnaire that follows will further contribute to your reflection and evaluation. Use it as a vital checkpoint on your way to your destination and follow the signposts provided by your knowledge and experience.

How and why to complete the questionnaire

In order to keep progressing with your CPD it is vital that you reflect on your progress so far. Often teachers I have worked with have said to me at this point, 'But I know what I've done and what I'm strong and weak in.' However, without dedicated reflection time it is very rare that this is truly the case. Quiet, focused time given over to real reflection brings up things that you might not even realise were there. It is always time well spent. The important thing is to note down your reflections and findings and make a plan of action going forward as a result of your musings.

You will remember the questionnaire process from chapter 2, but here is a reminder.

Quick response approach

If your preference for the self-evaluation is to go with your gut only, then simply fill in the quick response section after each question with the first thing that comes into your mind when you ask yourself the question. Do not mull over the question too carefully; simply read thoroughly and answer quickly. This approach will give you an overview of your current understanding and practice of using ICT and will take relatively little time. Just make sure you are uninterrupted, in a quiet place and able to complete the questionnaire in one sitting with no distractions so that you get focused and honest answers.

Considered response approach

If you choose to take a more reflective and detailed approach, then you can leave the quick response section blank and go straight on to reading the further guidance section under each question. This guidance provides prompt questions and ideas to get you thinking in detail about the question being answered and is designed to open up a wider scope in your answer. It will also enable you to look at your experience and pull examples into your answer to back up your statements. You may want to complete a few questions at a time and take breaks, or you may be prepared to sit and work through the questions all in one sitting to ensure you remain focused.

This approach does take longer, but it can lead to a more in-depth understanding of your current ICT practice, and you will gain more from the process than the quick response alone.

Combined approach

A thorough approach, and one I recommend, would be to use both approaches together regardless of personal preference. There is clear value in both approaches being used together. This would involve you firstly answering the self-evaluation quick response questions by briefly noting down your instinctual answers for all questions. The next step would be to return to the start of the self-evaluation, read the further guidance and then answer the questions once more, slowly and in detail forming more of a narrative around each question and pulling in examples

- I have done this self-assessment before.
- I only want a surface-level overview of my current understanding and practice.
- I work better when I work at speed.
- I don't have much time.

Quick

- I have never done this self-assessment before.
- I want a deeper understanding of my current understanding and practice.
- I work better when I take my time and really think things over.
- I have some time to do this self-assessment.

Considered

- I have never done this self-assessment before.
- I have done this self-assessment before.
- I want a comprehensive and full understanding of my current understanding and practice and want to compare that to what I thought before taking the self-assessment.
- I have a decent amount of time to dedicate to completing this self-assessment.

Combined

Fig. 7 How should I approach the self-assessment questionnaire?

from your own experience. Following this, you would need to read over both responses and form a comprehensive and honest summary in your mind of your answers and a final view of where you feel you stand right now in your CPD.

This is the longest of the three approaches to this questionnaire but will give you a comprehensive and full understanding of your current practice, thoughts and feelings in relation to using ICT in the classroom. You will be surprised at the difference you see between the quick response and the considered response answers to the same questions. It can be very illuminating.

Rate yourself

The final part of the self-evaluation is to rate yourself. This section will ask you to rate your confidence and happiness in each area that has been covered in the questionnaire with a view to working on these areas for improvement. The table below shows how the scale works: the higher the number you allocate yourself, the better you feel you are performing in that area.

Rating	Definition
1	Not at all. I don't. None at all. Not happy. Not confident at all.
2	Rarely. Barely. Very little. Very unconfident.
3	Not often at all. Not much. Quite unconfident.
4	Not particularly. Not really. Not a lot. Mildly unconfident.
5	Neutral. Unsure. Don't know. Indifferent.
6	Sometimes. At times. Moderately. A little bit. Mildly confident.
7	Quite often. A fair bit. Some. A little confident.
8	Most of the time. More often than not. Quite a lot. Quite confident.
9	The majority of the time. A lot. Very confident.
10	Completely. Very much so. A huge amount. Extremely happy. Extremely confident.

Fig. 8 Rate yourself definitions

Technology in the classroom: self-assessment questionnaire

QUESTION 1: What new things have you considered or tried that you have liked in terms of using technology in the classroom?

Quick response:

_____

_____

_____

_____

_____

Questions for consideration

- Did you use it for a specific purpose?
- Did it contribute to improved learning? How do you know?
- Did it make your job easier and/or more effective?

Considered response:

_____

_____

_____

_____

_____

Rate yourself

QUESTION 1: How happy are you that you've tried all you wanted to try using technology in the classroom?

1   2   3   4   5   6   7   8   9   10

QUESTION 2: What changes have you made that you feel have had an impact upon student attainment and achievement in your classroom?

Quick response:

_____

_____

_____

_____

_____

_____

Questions for consideration

- Did you consider that technology can impact both positively and negatively?
- What do your students think? What do they feel?
- What do other teachers think? What do they feel?

Considered response:

_____

_____

_____

_____

_____

_____

_____

Rate yourself

QUESTION 2: How much impact on student achievement and attainment do you feel the technology you've introduced has had?

| 1 | 2 | 3 | 4 | 5 | 6 | 7 | 8 | 9 | 10 |

QUESTION 3: How would you now describe your general approach to using technology and how it has changed?

Quick response:

_____

_____

_____

_____

_____

_____

Questions for consideration

- Are you using technology for the sake of using technology or are you using it to fulfil a pedagogical purpose?
- Have you explored the latest pedagogical theories? How familiar are you with research findings?
- How does what you know about great teaching and learning intersect with technology?

Considered response:

_____

_____

_____

_____

_____

_____

Rate yourself

QUESTION 3: How happy are you with your approach to using technology in the classroom?

| 1 | 2 | 3 | 4 | 5 | 6 | 7 | 8 | 9 | 10 |

QUESTION 4: What educational theories, research, ideas or case studies do you have an interest in and how do they inform your practice?

Quick response:

_____

_____

_____

_____

_____

_____

Questions for consideration

- How do the case studies in chapter 5 correspond with your own experience?
- Where would you place yourself in the spectrum from traditional to progressive? How does technology support or challenge your approach to education?
- How are your own ideal and beliefs reflected more widely? Are your colleagues more likely to follow your lead or react defensively?

Considered response:

_____

_____

_____

_____

_____

_____

Rate yourself

QUESTION 4: How confident are you with your knowledge of educational research?

1   2   3   4   5   6   7   8   9   10

QUESTION 5: What have you shared or discussed regarding using technology with colleagues outside your department?

Quick response:

_____

_____

_____

_____

_____

_____

Questions for consideration

- Are your discussions focused on technology or pedagogy?
- Are there frequent opportunities for discussion? Do discussions happen formally or informally?
- How successful would you say you have been in communicating your vision and purpose for the use of technology?

Considered response:

_____

_____

_____

_____

_____

_____

Rate yourself

QUESTION 5: How confident are you about sharing your ideas with others on a whole-school level?

1	2	3	4	5	6	7	8	9	10

QUESTION 6: What have you shared or discussed regarding technology with colleagues in your department?

Quick response:

_____
_____
_____
_____
_____
_____
_____

Questions for consideration

- Are departmental meetings focused on administration or sharing practice?
- How does technology fit with your colleagues' educational philosophy?
- What are you personally doing to win hearts and minds?

Considered response:

_____
_____
_____
_____
_____
_____
_____

Rate yourself

QUESTION 6: How confident are you about sharing your ideas with others on a departmental level?

1   2   3   4   5   6   7   8   9   10

QUESTION 7: Where do you feel your strengths now lie in using technology in the classroom?

Quick response:

_____

_____

_____

_____

_____

_____

Questions for consideration

- Do you feel your practice is better informed?
- What do you find harder, knowing when to use technology or knowing when not to?
- Are your students learning better because of your use of technology? How do you know?

Considered response:

_____

_____

_____

_____

_____

_____

_____

Rate yourself

QUESTION 7: How confident are you when it comes to your technology practice?

| 1 | 2 | 3 | 4 | 5 | 6 | 7 | 8 | 9 | 10 |

QUESTION 8: Where do you feel your weaknesses now lie when using technology in the classroom?

Quick response:

_____

_____

_____

_____

_____

_____

_____

Questions for consideration

- Do these weaknesses stem from a lack of technological or pedagogical knowledge?
- Have you and your colleagues carried out mutual lesson observations and feedback?
- Have you sought to gather views from colleagues and students?

Considered response:

_____

_____

_____

_____

_____

_____

Rate yourself

QUESTION 8: How serious do you feel your weaknesses are when it comes to using technology in the classroom?

1   2   3   4   5   6   7   8   9   10

QUESTION 9: What approaches would you like to try that you have not already?

Quick response:

_____

_____

_____

_____

_____

_____

_____

Questions for consideration

- Is your focus on more use of technology or better use of technology?
- What have you learnt from the student voice and discussions with colleagues?
- What changes or additions to your classroom or setting would help you achieve a more effective use of technology?

Considered response:

_____

_____

_____

_____

_____

_____

Rate yourself

QUESTION 9: How confident are you when it comes to trying something new when using technology?

| 1 | 2 | 3 | 4 | 5 | 6 | 7 | 8 | 9 | 10 |

QUESTION 10: Is there anything that is holding you back in developing your use of technology in the classroom?

Quick response:

_____

_____

_____

_____

_____

_____

Questions for consideration

- What areas of development have you identified for yourself? What about for your colleagues?
- Do you feel well supported by your line manager and your school's senior leadership?
- Is the technology that is available fit for purpose?

Considered response:

_____

_____

_____

_____

_____

_____

_____

Rate yourself

QUESTION 10: How confident do you feel that you are not being held back?

1	2	3	4	5	6	7	8	9	10

QUESTION 11: Is there anything that you have tried in the classroom as a result of using this book so far?

Quick response:

_____

_____

_____

_____

_____

_____

_____

Questions for consideration

- How have the strategies and case studies reviewed in this book informed your practice?
- What has worked well for you and what hasn't? Why?
- How do you intend to cascade what you have learnt?

Considered response:

_____

_____

_____

_____

_____

_____

_____

Rate yourself

QUESTION 11: How confident do you feel in trying out new approaches with technology?

| 1 | 2 | 3 | 4 | 5 | 6 | 7 | 8 | 9 | 10 |

QUESTION 12: Do you have an understanding of what students think about your use of technology?

Quick response:

_____

_____

_____

_____

_____

_____

Questions for consideration

- How do students view technology? Do they associate it with academic purposes? Why or why not?
- Are you relying on students spontaneously learning how to use the technology effectively or have you dedicated time and effort to teach them?
- Have students' views informed your use of technology? How?

Considered response:

_____

_____

_____

_____

_____

_____

_____

Rate yourself

QUESTION 12: How confident are you that you really know what students think about your use of technology?

1   2   3   4   5   6   7   8   9   10

QUESTION 13: How have you interacted with your students in terms of using technology in the classroom?

Quick response:

_____

_____

_____

_____

_____

_____

Questions for consideration

- Who uses technology most in lessons, you or your students? How do you feel about the ratio? How about your students?
- How would more technology help or hinder their learning?
- Is technology a distraction or an aid for them?

Considered response:

_____

_____

_____

_____

_____

_____

_____

_____

Rate yourself

QUESTION 13: How confident are you when it comes to using technology with students?

| 1 | 2 | 3 | 4 | 5 | 6 | 7 | 8 | 9 | 10 |

QUESTION 14: How have you interacted with parents and carers about the technology you're using in class?

Quick response:

_____
_____
_____
_____
_____
_____

Questions for consideration

- Are parents or carers aware of your vision and purpose regarding the use of technology in the classroom? How do you know this?
- Have parents or carers been given specific examples of technology use in lessons? Are they supportive of your efforts?
- Have you ever sought parents' or carers' views about the use of technology?

Considered response:

_____
_____
_____
_____
_____
_____

Rate yourself

QUESTION 14: How confident are you that you know what parents think about your use of technology?

1   2   3   4   5   6   7   8   9   10

The results

Great job. Your honesty in responding to these questions and in your reflection is paramount to making progress and tailoring an action plan for your own professional development and that of your colleagues. From now on you need to think more seriously about leading the professional development of others. Part 2 of this book will help you with this, but the starting point may well differ considerably according to your context.

Reflect on how you rated your answers for each question in the questionnaire and compare your ratings with the chart below, which will guide you to taking the next steps in your planning for the use of technology in the classroom.

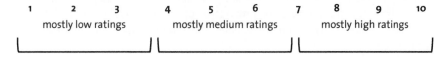

Fig. 9 How did you rate yourself?

Mostly low ratings

The use of technology in your context faces some serious challenges but these are surmountable with the right investment and support. There will be hard lessons to be learnt along the way but you are well-placed to meet these challenges. Your programme of training and ongoing communication and support should probably focus on developing and embedding a vision for the use of technology, firmly grounding this in sound pedagogical practices.

Mostly medium ratings

Technology is present in your context but it may benefit from a more explicit connection to pedagogy. You and your colleagues may view technology as useful but not essential to the delivery of lessons and the facilitation of learning, thus relegating technology and technology CPD to the lower divisions of school priorities. Move forward with a focus on highlighting the strong connection between great teaching and effective use of technology.

Mostly high ratings

Technology is well embedded in your setting, and teachers and students use it habitually to support the daily business of teaching and learning. There are areas for development and maybe even pockets of resistance, but overall everyone accepts that the effective application of technology can support great teaching and learning. As you plan ahead, focus on moving the use of technology forward by making explicit what can now be done with technology that you and your colleagues couldn't do before. The conceptual models in chapter 1 should help you with this.

Now what?

Use the results of this questionnaire to inform the next stage of your implementation. As your confidence grows in the use of technology and in your knowledge of the pedagogical reasons why and when it should be applied, you will be ready to start devising a more detailed training plan so that you can begin to start training others. Please don't miss this opportunity to reflect and really interrogate yourself about your knowledge of and your motives for the use of technology.

Chapter 6 takeaway

Teaching tip

Be transparent with your colleagues, your students and their parents. Share goals and success criteria. Like any good teacher knows, progress is only made if those learning from them know where they are, where they are going to and how they are getting there. This applies to you just as well.

Pass it on

By now you should have considered seriously the possibility of sharing your knowledge and practice digitally, illustrating what makes great teaching and learning with technology using technological tools. There is nothing wrong with the odd sheet, but if your colleagues see you relying on paper to teach and train them, they will think, even if only subconsciously, that you're good at talking the talk but less good at walking the walk. Keep a digital record of your findings: shared folders with key documents, webpages or teaching and learning blogs are all great ways to exemplify the principles and strategies that you have read about thus far in this book.

Share and tweet

Twitter is one of these digital ways to share your practice. Encourage your colleagues to join your 'personal learning network' online. Use the hashtag #BloomsCPD to link thread-related tweets and keep track of the conversation as it develops.

CPD book club

'Principles of instruction' by Barak Rosenshine is not a book, but it packs a huge amount of knowledge and wisdom about great teaching in a very readable article format (see the Bibliography for full details).

Blogger's corner

Larry Cuban is a veteran blogger, education technologist and Professor Emeritus of Education at Stanford University. His blog is a must read for teachers seeking to learn about the effective application of technology to support learning. Larry blogs here: https://larrycuban.wordpress.com

TO DO LIST:

- ❏ Leave some time after completing your questionnaire and then reread your answers to reflect more deeply about their significance
- ❏ Consider any areas that, as a result of the questionnaire, you now wish to focus on or need to work on
- ❏ Tweet your main reflections and conclusions from the questionnaire using the hashtag #BloomsCPD
- ❏ Discuss the questionnaire questions with your colleagues next time you meet as a department or team
- ❏ Visit and bookmark Larry Cuban's blog
- ❏ Read the report 'Principles of instruction'

7

Evaluating progress beyond the individual

By now you should have a better understanding of what effective use of technology to support teaching and learning means in practice. If, ultimately, transforming teaching practice is your main objective, I suggest that you shift your focus towards curricula and pedagogy instead, as introducing more technology is unlikely to transform anything for the better just by itself. Technology can indeed change how we teach and learn, but this is usually a process – not an event – and is more likely to happen over time when it supports well-established teaching practice.

And herein lies the difficulty in evaluating progress when adopting new technologies. Teaching is a complex beast with numerous variables in place. Pinning down success to a particular intervention can be fiendishly difficult to achieve. In this chapter, we will explore ways in which we begin to evaluate what positive or negative impact technology has over time, in the knowledge that improved results are just one of the measures at our disposal and that not everything that counts can be counted. As such, we will look at ways in which we can use proxy indicators that can be linked to progress. Instead of just asking 'what is technology's impact?', we will ask 'what is technology's impact for X purpose in Y context?'

Key questions for reflection

What is the problem you are trying to solve?

The introduction of new technologies in schools is often associated with providing a solution for a perceived problem. This approach is much sounder than simply being attracted moth-like by the 21st-century flame without much thought about implications down the line, such as ongoing budget commitments, professional development requirements or, lest we forget, actual impact on learning. However, it is crucial that you, your colleagues and your students are satisfied, on the one hand, that there is a problem to be solved and, on the other, that technology is the best solution to solve it.

Plans, strategies, solutions and ideas that make perfect sense in your head can suddenly develop obvious flaws the moment they are exposed to other people. Sound out your ideas with colleagues and students. Do not work in splendid isolation but, instead, surround yourself with colleagues who you can trust to tell you what you need to hear, not what you want to hear. Above all, be unfailingly humble and learn from the vast amount of knowledge and wisdom of those around you.

How do you know whether things are going well?

- Consider the opportunity cost of your technology implementation. If time, effort and money are going to be invested in it, where are time, effort and money being diverted from to turn your ideas into reality? Is this diversion negating any advantages that may be gained from the technology?
- Write a rationale for your proposed technology intervention describing the problem as you see it and how your solution can contribute to ameliorating it or even solving it.
- Share your rationale with a trusted group of colleagues whose opinions you value, even if you don't always agree with them – in fact, especially if you don't always agree with them. Colleagues from a varied cross-section of the school who can bring on board different perspectives would be most useful – subject leaders, pastoral leaders, learning support staff, NQTs, more experienced teachers and SLT.
- Seek constructive feedback and critique from your colleagues. Arrange regular meetings in which you dedicate time to discuss and develop a shared understanding of the issues, the proposed solutions and how the reality of the technology implementation is shaping up. Whilst potential misconceptions do need to be clarified, don't be defensive in the face of criticism, but rather flexible and reflective.
- Depending on the technology intervention, you may want to repeat the above process with a focus group of students (see below).

Do teachers think progress is being made?

The old joke about changing practice in complex organisations goes like this: when asked *who wants **change**?* almost everyone's hands go up. However, when asked *who wants **to change**?* hardly any hands go up. This is because by and large change is effortful. As the person responsible for introducing change, it can be easy to forget that you are also responsible for adding grease to the mill.

Once your rationale has been reviewed, critiqued and improved by a select group of colleagues, you are ready to present this rationale to the wider staff body, making clear what the benefits to their practice and the students' learning will be. Provide opportunities for colleagues to adopt the technology and create an atmosphere in which trying things out is allowed and in which mistakes can be made safely, all the time trusting teachers and their professional judgement to never jeopardise learning and progress. Some things will work better than others in different contexts for different people. Other things won't work at all. This information will be very valuable and you should not dismiss all negative feedback as simple nay-saying, although some might well be!

How do you know whether things are going well?

- The professional development required to embed change successfully in the longer term is often neglected in favour of more immediate, flash-in-the-pan approaches. You should avoid falling into this trap and assume that the organisation of frequent professional development opportunities for colleagues (regular lunchtime or twilight sessions, for example) are a must. Use these opportunities to evaluate levels of adoption, gauge the mood and inform the ongoing implementation in a two-way street. It's not just about what change you are making, but also about how your approach is changing in response.
- Craft a cross-sectional anonymous survey that provides you with results that are as high in granularity as possible. You will need to know what is working, for whom (focus not on identity, but rather on subject taught, level of experience, age, etc) and why. Crucially, you will also need to know what isn't working, for whom and why.
- Conduct interviews with colleagues. Use these as an opportunity to get to the bottom of issues that may have arisen. Why did something not work? Why did something work? What factors were involved in each instance of failure or successful adoption?

Do students think progress is being made?

An erroneous assumption often made by technology advocates is that children will just love digital technology simply by dint of being digital. It is true to an extent. Children do naturally like a bit of novelty and play. However, conversely, they are also rather better than we sometimes give them credit for at identifying when something is a fruitful addition to their learning environment or just a gimmick. If something is just a bit of fun with a few bells and whistles attached they will welcome it to begin with, but they will be the first to throw a bucket of shockingly cold water on your best intentions with a 'not that again, Miss' if you assume that just fun, bells and whistles are what students expect. For most, it's not. Above all else, the majority of students want to learn and feel that they are making progress. Although, let's be clear: enjoyment and learning are certainly not mutually exclusive.

If your technology implementation involves a different experience for students, such as access to online resources or setting and tracking homework, then you should involve your students from the outset. Please don't assume students like change more than adults. They absolutely don't. Your rationale will need to be explained to them just as clearly and, just like the adults, they will need to understand what the problem is and why the solution helps before they are ready to consider your proposals seriously.

How do you know whether things are going well?

- Appoint student Digital Leaders and meet with them like you would with colleagues. Make them part of your planning and implementation. Listen to their concerns, hopes and expectations so that you can ameliorate, shape and manage them as required. And, of course, take on board their advice when applicable.
- Arrange with pastoral leaders for Digital Leaders to be given the opportunity to explain in their own words to other students what the implementation is about. This could be done in form time, year assemblies or whole school assemblies.
- Once the implementation is underway, survey all your students to gauge reaction. Once again craft your survey for maximum granularity: for which year group is the implementation working/not working? Which subjects are having more success/problems? Why? Avoid asking general questions about technology such as *'Do you like technology?'* and consider making statements for students to select their agreement or disagreement on a scale. For example:

I have greater access to online resources

Strongly agree – Agree – Neither agree nor disagree – Disagree – Strongly agree

or

I receive more frequent feedback from my teachers

Strongly agree – Agree – Neither agree nor disagree – Disagree – Strongly agree

but also questions such as

Access to online resources makes me more likely to get distracted on the internet

Strongly agree – Agree – Neither agree nor disagree – Disagree – Strongly agree

Is progress being made on outcomes?

For many people, this is the only measure that counts. They would ask: if a huge deal of time, effort and money is being invested in an initiative that then doesn't result in improved outcomes, will it have been a failure? Is an improvement in examination results the only valid proxy for success? Unfortunately, there are no right answers to these questions because they are the wrong questions.

Successful technology implementations can deliver transformation in the medium to long term, but in the short term are all about the marginal gains. Take mobile telephony. In its inception, a clunky device housed in your car (hence its original name *Carphone*), allowed you to make and receive mobile phone calls. A string of subtle marginal gains – gradual reduction in size; introduction of text messaging; access to the internet; app development – have resulted years later in the powerful, portable, multipurpose device that is probably within a one-metre radius of your person as you read this chapter and which has proven its utility to you for so many purposes.

The success of the original mobile phones could only be measured by their ability to make mobile phone calls and so the ability of your technology implementation should be measured on its ability to tackle whichever problem you set out to solve or ameliorate in the first place, rather than on its ability to improve education all by itself in the short term. Clearly examination results do matter and it is possible that a drop in exam results could be linked to your intervention. The message here is that exam results are important but that they should not be seen as the only proxy for success.

How do you know whether things are going well?

- Identify proxies that can help you triangulate and determine whether an intervention is having a positive effect. Test and exam results are valid proxies, but so are qualitative judgements on whether the processes involved in teaching and learning are enhanced, and general levels of satisfaction with the implementation. If teachers or students feel that the implementation has been successful, the likelihood is that it has been, even if examination results have not improved discernibly in the short term.
- Devise a questionnaire for your surveys and interviews that can be reused at regular intervals to allow you to measure progress over time. You will be essentially asking the same questions and measuring how judgements and attitudes related to your implementation of technology change.

Chapter 7 takeaway

Teaching tip

As they say, 'If you want to make enemies, try to change something.' Being the deliverer of change can be rewarding and frustrating in equal measure. The most important piece of advice I can give you is to always take on board the opinions of others. When faced with a harsh critique or opposition, don't be dismissive, but accepting. Don't be argumentative, but emollient. And, above all, be reflective.

Whilst we all see the merit in our own ideas and interventions, we are often less keen to accept the views of others or to acknowledge that things may have taken a wrong turn somewhere. The people around you – colleagues and students – will respect you more and be more supportive of the initiative if you are able to demonstrate leadership by being reflective and having the strength to change course and take advice when good advice is given.

Pass it on

When tasked with the responsibility to devise a new implementation, it is too easy to fall into the trap of feeling that you are responsible for reinventing the wheel. Take a step back and remember that the wheel you are working on has probably been invented elsewhere many times over. Apple, Microsoft and Google all run programmes that recognise, celebrate and share technological expertise among teachers. Involve yourself in these communities and consider applying to become an active member.

Share and tweet

Reach out to the well-established community of practitioners on Twitter, LinkedIn and Facebook. Share your experiences with them. Use the hashtag #BloomsCPD where possible.

CPD book club

Visible Learning and the Science of How We Learn is the work of John Hattie and Gregory Yates and explores the strategies and methods that have been shown to maximise achievement in schools. The book's premise is that if schools and teachers know their impact, they will become more effective. We can take this further by entertaining the notion that teachers who are well informed about what makes for great teaching and learning will be better able to plan and implement interventions based on the adoption of educational technology.

Blogger's corner

Dominic Norrish is director of technology at United Learning, a large group of academies and independent schools in the UK. He has done a huge deal of work on researching and measuring the impact of technology on education. He blogs at www.domnorrish.com.

To do list:

- ☐ Share the rationale for your implementation with colleagues and reflect carefully on their feedback
- ☐ Devise questionnaires, schedule meetings and plan interviews that will allow you to make a judgement on what impact your implementation is having
- ☐ Familiarise yourself with software that allows you to craft surveys and questionnaires. Both Google for Education and Microsoft's Office 365 have a forms tool that is excellent for this purpose
- ☐ Reach out to and become a member of online communities of practice
- ☐ Read *Visible Learning and the Science of How We Learn*
- ☐ Visit Dominic Norrish's blog

Part 2

Train others

1

Planning and preparing your training

One of the most successful ways in which teachers can improve their practice is through their participation in continuing professional development (CPD) programmes. However, we've all attended INSET and external CPD events once or twice a year in which, ironically ignoring everything we know about how learning best takes place, we cram a clearly overwhelming amount of information into a day of glorious perplexity and incertitude. Is it any wonder then that such events often generate more scepticism than enthusiasm?

I remember when I organised a whole staff INSET that was to be delivered on the first day of term, after my school had supplied iPads to all the teachers. The focus of the INSET was on using iPads effectively in lessons and it was delivered by a former teacher who had become a specialist Apple trainer. The day was scheduled so that iPad functionality could be explored, in theory introducing teachers to the gamut of new possibilities now available to them.

However, in hindsight, I failed to take our context into account and happily organised for the same INSET programme to be delivered to reception teachers all the way through to sixth form specialists. Large chunks of the INSET were dedicated to trialling some of the different apps that were available. One of these apps was a tool that allowed students to create animations using on-screen puppets, which could be recorded and submitted in class or as homework. After one hour of playing with puppets on an iPad's screen it became clear that Year 4 teachers were by and large excited and eager to put what they had learnt into practice with their pupils, but also that my colleagues who taught economics in the sixth form were considering putting an end to it all. Hindsight, as they say, is 20/20.

In this chapter, we will explore what makes great CPD, as well as what the unique challenges are of organising technology-focused training for teachers. In addition, we will catch the briefest of glimpses into the psychology behind human behaviour and how this may affect how your CPD is received and, ultimately, the success of the technology implementation.

What makes great CPD?

We can all agree that effective CPD should inform and improve our practice. When planning a CPD programme, consider the following:

- What is the purpose of training teachers? Is there a shared sense of purpose? Are teachers happy about receiving the training or do they view it as unnecessary?
- What are the needs of the teachers in front of you? Make the training relevant to their practice and their daily experience of teaching in a classroom.

- Would you deliver material to your pupils as a one-off, never to be revisited? Then why would you do it in a CPD session? Focus instead on spacing out the training so that it takes place over time, preferably throughout an academic year as a minimum, revisiting concepts and tools periodically during this time.

Perhaps the most important consideration, however, is that you should not embark on this planning process alone. Be affiliative and involve colleagues who can help you with both the planning and delivery of this programme. And hang a welcome sign on your door, keeping it open so that colleagues continue to join you as the programme unfolds.

Top tips for running technology CPD

Running technology CPD brings its own unique challenges, some of which are foreseeable, but others may well have the potential to catch you by surprise:

- **Wider than usual variance in teacher aptitude.** Technology is one of those things in life – like not being good at maths – that many people feel a degree of pride in when stating their inadequacy with a shrug of their shoulders. And so some of your colleagues will be very technology-savvy but many others may need to start with the most basic training. It is crucial therefore to avoid the one-size-fits-all approach to CPD and build in differentiation into your CPD programme. It would be a good idea for you to offer one-to-one sessions to your most technologically-challenged colleagues.
- **Reluctance to participate.** Technology is often seen as a not always welcome addition to the classroom: a luxury that is not really necessary at best or a hindrance to learning at worst. Section off parts of your CPD programme and dedicate them to explaining the whys and wherefores of the technology implementation. Illustrate your points with plenty of examples of the technology in action, achieving the purpose you set out to achieve.
- **Temptation to make the training all about the technology.** Avoid delivering sessions that are all about learning to use specific bits of technology. There is nothing more tedious than guiding a large group of people through basic functionality, such us how to open an account or how to log in. Instead send out these details in advance and, during the session, focus on the intersection between technology and pedagogy, highlighting how the technology can help achieve specific pedagogical purposes, with built-in opportunities of initial practice for participants.
- **Does the technology actually work?** I don't mean this in a pedagogical sense, but rather in the sense of technology actually turning on and operating as intended. Double check and triple check that the technology your CPD session is built around is working well. Get your IT support team to perform a check

on the technology at the venue. Don't be fobbed off with an 'It should work' – either it works or it doesn't. Be exacting. There is nothing worse than starting a CPD session on technology in which the technology fails at the outset, with someone quipping 'That's technology for you!' Technology should work, and it is the ICT support team's job to ensure that it does.

- **Forgetting about the children and their parents.** The easiest thing in the world (that 20/20 hindsight again) is to forget about the children, or worse: to believe that as children of the digital age they are somehow born with innate digital powers that negate any requirement to introduce the technology and its pedagogical purpose, and train them as you would the teachers. Don't assume this. You will need to train them too, especially if you are rolling out the kind of technology that involves heavy student use, such as mobile devices (including Bring Your Own Device schemes) or new virtual learning environments. Consider also keeping the parents informed throughout the programme via newsletters or even information evenings.

In-house vs external CPD

External CPD can get a bad rap. Quite justifiably sometimes, as neither parachuting someone in to school for a day nor being sent away from school on your own for a course tend to result in the kind of long-term positive impact that is more securely associated with CPD programmes that are sustained over a period of time. This doesn't mean that external CPD providers should be ignored, just that their participation needs to be built in throughout the programme, not just in one burst right at the beginning.

If you are purchasing a digital resource, then negotiate a sustained commitment to the provision and participation in a long-term CPD, preferably locking it in on the contract. Apple, Google and Microsoft all have certified trainers that you can draw on. Major educational technology providers will also employ or at the very least be able to recommend specialists that have experience of school implementations. Use them initially to train your group of digital champions – the folks who have been identified as potential allies, helpers and ambassadors for the technology implementations – and then as part of a wider staff CPD programme, alternating between sessions that are led by colleagues (most) and external trainers (fewer).

Chapter 2 will focus more on providing session ideas and training plans, but you may want to start thinking already about how you may be able to weave this CPD programme into your school's *business-as-usual*:

- **INSET.** Negotiate time allocated to training staff during termly INSET with your school's senior leadership. These are good times to bring in external trainers, should they be available or should you require them, or to run a carousel led by you and your digital champions.
- **Lunchtime and twilight sessions.** Publish a programme of regular lunchtime and twilight sessions, ideally differentiated so that they attract participants of similar levels of aptitude or expertise.
- **Briefing takeover.** With your senior leaders' blessing, of course. Propose to them the need to dedicate a briefing to updating teachers on the progress made or to further illustrate how the technology should be used or, hopefully, how it is being used.
- **Residency.** One idea that has worked really well in schools is to invite a specialist trainer to take residence periodically in the staffroom for three to five days. This facilitates a more *ad-hoc* approach in which teachers spend quality one-to-one time with the trainer when they have a minute, perhaps over a coffee. Heads of department can also invite the trainer to their departmental meetings to discuss the technology implementation in context. This may sound like an expensive luxury, but it may be offered at no extra cost if negotiated at the time of signing a contract or terms of purchase, for example.
- **TeachMeets.** These are informal gatherings of teachers, generally after school or at the weekend, in which interested teachers – not just from your school – come together to share and discuss practice. Usually teachers volunteer to speak for a short time about a resource or an approach they have adopted. Not everyone is a speaker; folks are welcome to attend simply to watch and take note. Regular TeachMeets can be particularly successful if themed (e.g. technology) and organised in cooperation with other schools, taking turns as hosts.

Chapter 1 takeaway

Teaching tip

How human beings make and justify their decisions is a fascinating area of study. Psychologists have long warned about our proclivity to fall prey to irrational decision-making, logical fallacies, prejudice and bias, which often determine why new ideas are adopted. Psychology has shown that we instinctively place more importance on our own ideas than on those of others. It's a well-documented psychological phenomenon called the *Not Invented Here Bias*. This bias suggests that your idea could be rejected by others simply because it is not their idea, and not on its actual merit.

This suggests that you should consider carefully how your message is being delivered to colleagues:

- Be humble and avoid sounding as if you know best. Even if you do know best about the technology, you may not be as familiar with how technology is applied in a particular subject or context.
- Challenge misconceptions decisively but considerately. Show that you understand the root of the misconception. Treat anything that you might believe to be a misconception as an opportunity to learn about where your colleagues are coming from. And always remember that you too are prone to misconceptions.
- Don't be prescriptive. Describe instead the technology use in broad strokes, focusing on how it supports learning and providing opportunities for colleagues to connect the dots so that a picture of how the technology might work in their context emerges in their own minds.

I have often heard colleagues quip that one of the best ways to get school leadership to adopt your idea is to craftily make it look as if it was their own. It turns out that this is backed up by science!

Pass it on

TeachMeets work really well when colleagues attend from a variety of schools. However, there is no reason why you should not plan a series of termly or half-termly TeachMeets focusing on your own colleagues in school. TeachMeets are excellent ways to share practice in an informal environment. TeachMeets can be great fun: order pizza, bring cake and, when there are no children on site, maybe even a few beers. If your technology implementation is the result of a large purchase, your technology supplier may be willing to provide sponsorship in the form of goodies and treats to persuade colleagues to attend.

CPD book club

The Teacher Development Trust has conducted research on the provision of CPD and has identified the features that characterise effective CPD: http://tdtrust.org/about/evidence

Blogger's corner

Not a blogger as such, Dan Ariely is a psychologist and writer who occasionally publishes articles and talks on his website. Dan has spent his career studying the irrationality behind most of the human behaviour. Read Dan's work and watch some of his talks for a glimpse into how humans make decisions: http://danariely.com

TO DO LIST:

☐ Reflect about what makes great CPD

☐ Begin discussing your plans for a sustained CPD programme with senior colleagues

☐ Organise an initial TeachMeet-style event in support of your technology implementation. Remember to focus it on pedagogy, with technology providing the backgroud

☐ Tweet about the progress you are making in planning a sustained programmed of CPD. Use the hashtag #BloomsCPD

☐ Learn about human psychology to help you improve your CPD provision. Exploring Dan Ariely's website is a good start

☐ Read about what researchers have found about effective CPD in the Teacher Development Trust's website

2 Training plans

Having reviewed the principles of great CPD in the previous chapter, we will now explore ways in which staff training on technology can be practically and successfully delivered. Our focus will not be on one-off INSET sessions – although, if available, they should be added to the training programme – but rather on continuous and regularly spaced out opportunities to improve your colleagues' awareness and knowledge about the technology that has been made available.

We will begin by proposing five quick and easy training sessions, 15 minutes in length, that you or a colleague could deliver in a staff briefing or to a department over a lunch break, for example. These are designed to be concise and practical: one technology-based strategy and how it could be used in practice. For the purposes of illustration, I will base these quick and easy sessions on the case studies we examined in chapter 5, but you should consider what technology is available in your setting and adapt these plans accordingly.

Finally, we will look at the planning of a further five twilight sessions for CPD of approximately one hour in duration, to be delivered after school over the course of an academic year. It is important that these sessions have a more explicit pedagogic focus and so they will explore how the use of technology can support and enhance the processes involved in teaching and learning. In other words, they ought to be less about the *tech* and more about the *teach*.

15-minute sessions:

1. Digital learning spaces
2. Modelling using a visualiser
3. Giving feedback using technology
4. Collaborating using office tools
5. Online quizzes

Twilight sessions:

1. An introduction to using technology in the classroom
2. Improving classroom instruction using the principles of dual coding
3. Exploring the principles of interleaving topics and spacing study
4. Encouraging learners to plan, monitor and evaluate their own learning
5. The secret powers of testing

15-minute session 1: Digital learning spaces

Introduction to training

In contexts where some or most of the content is stored in digital format, it pays to make sure that colleagues understand the utility for students of being able to access resources whenever and wherever they are. Yes, many of them may prefer printed materials, but when these aren't available (left in a locker, eaten by the dog...), content in digital format becomes very handy because it is ubiquitously available and virtually *unloseable*.

The temptation to be avoided is to spend the short time available showing colleagues how to use the technology, whether it's a content management system, a virtual learning environment or whichever other way of making content available to students your school or department has invested in. Instead, put your teachers in the students' shoes and demonstrate how a degree of *blended learning* (combining digital media with more traditional classroom methods) could be brought about using this kind of tool. Focus on how students interact with the content and how useful and convenient it is *for the students*.

Preparation and resources required

- Familiarise yourself with the technology that will facilitate *blended learning* and the digital sharing of content.
- Prepare content in advance for participants to access. You could use existing content if available or you may want to create a sample unit of work for demonstration purposes, complete with multimedia content (e.g. embedded video), worksheets or whichever resources you deem may be suitable.
- Book a suitable space for the training to happen. The venue should have projection facilities and speakers.
- If your school provides teachers with laptops, tablets or any other kind of mobile technology, you should request that participants bring them to the training. If not, book a computer suite, so that each participant has access to a computer during the session.
- Share a summary of the main points covered in the session in Word or PDF by email before the session. Alternatively, you may want to be bold and make a brief audio or video recording instead, which could then be shared.
- If you have student digital champions in place, they would be an asset during the session, providing a student voice. If not, enlist the help of willing students to help you demonstrate the capabilities of the technology.

Step-by-step instructions

- Start with a brief overview of the content sharing technology (such as virtual learning environments, online content management systems, or even shared folders and drives): how do students use it? When did students find it useful? Why do they find it useful? *(2–5 minutes)*
- Either get your colleagues to join a class or space you have set up online or demonstrate using enlisted students sitting among the teachers. Demonstrate how resources are accessed by students and how tasks are set, completed and received using the technology. *(9–10 minutes)*
- Provide participants with a brief takeaway guide outlining the pedagogical benefits of sharing content digitally, brief instructions covering how to use the technology and where to get further help, and a huge deal of encouragement.

Potential concern from teachers

My students and I prefer paper. Making resources available digitally simply adds to my workload.

Students may well prefer paper. The point here is that resources are available to students whenever and wherever they require them. If students wish to print them, that will be up to them, but by making them available online you have removed any potential for loss or misplacement of resources. The student voice on this is very positive: they may well like paper, but they would rather have seamless access to material whenever required. We don't have to choose between what's preferable and what's more easily available; we can have both.

15-minute session 2: Modelling using a visualiser

Introduction to training

Visualisers tend to be a quick win because they fit seamlessly into already-established traditional practice and because they are relatively cheap. A range of affordable desktop visualisers are available, but the same principles apply if, for example, you are using a tablet that allows you to relay its screen to the main projector, either wirelessly (e.g. Chromecast or AirPlay) or by wiring it directly to the projector. Teachers are usually quick to realise the utility of being able to model student work as it is being produced, thus allowing them to capture and clarify misconceptions before they have time to embed them, and modelling excellence and high attainment.

Once again, I would avoid sessions that focus on learning to operate the equipment. Instead plan a session that demonstrates how the technology can be used to enable progress to be made at a faster pace. The best way to achieve this is to teach the participants something new.

Preparation and resources required

- Learn to operate the desktop visualiser. If you are using a tablet or other mobile device, ensure the projector can receive a video feed from the tablet.
- Pick a topic that you are very familiar with (you may resort to your subject specialism or you may wish to lighten the mood and choose something fun and unlikely).
- Plan a 'lesson' that involves participants developing answers on paper.
- Book a suitable venue with projection facilities for your training.
- Prepare a how-to document that participants can take away after the session.

Step-by-step instructions

- Start by introducing the benefits of modelling student work during a lesson, e.g. dispelling misconceptions or showcasing excellence. (2–5 minutes)
- Introduce your chosen topic for the demonstration. (2–3 minutes)
- Provide participants with a question about your topic for them to answer in writing, maybe in pairs or small groups. Give them two minutes.
- Pick at least two pieces of work then project them to the participants using the visualising equipment. Challenge participants to provide commentary in the 'What Went Well' / 'Even Better If' format and write any suggestions, corrections or improvements on screen using any in-built annotation tools or just a marker pen if projection onto a whiteboard. (6–8 minutes)
- Provide participants with a quick-read, takeaway guide to the pedagogical benefits of visualisers, as well as information about where to get further help from if required.

Potential concern from teachers

Technology is often unreliable. I'd much rather stick to other methods that don't rely on technology.

This is a very valid concern. Technology is meant to facilitate processes, not make them harder. Any potential technology introduction will need to be carefully supported by your IT support team, who will need to make sure that any technology works like the lights work when you turn the switch or like water flows when you turn the tap. You and your IT support team will need to work hard to increase teacher confidence. Hopefully enough teachers will begin to use visualisers to allow for the word to spread, contributing to greater confidence among your colleagues.

15-minute session 3: Giving feedback using technology

Introduction to training

Giving feedback ought to be integral to teaching, not an additional intervention. Great teaching is characterised by the successful ascertaining of where the student is, where she needs to go and how to get there. Technology can help with this process mainly by providing alternative ways to provide feedback (e.g. video or audio recordings) or improving the timeliness of its receipt.

Therefore, the session ought to focus on the pedagogical impact of timely feedback and on exploring ways to reduce teacher workload. Finding quick wins for often overworked teachers ought to be a priority for these quick and easy sessions.

Preparation and resources required

- Familiarise yourself with the technology you have chosen to provide feedback. This could be a virtual learning environment or a classroom management tool such as Google Classroom or Showbie.
- Choose a sample piece of work submitted by a student or make it more entertaining by choosing a topical newspaper or magazine article.
- Think about what feedback could be given that would cause students to think and work harder than the person giving feedback. The focus should be on enabling progress by setting challenging goals that take students just beyond their current level of achievement.
- Book a suitable venue for the session. Projection facilities and speakers (especially if you will be demonstrating audio feedback) are a must.
- Prepare a takeaway guide summarising the main points covered during the session.

Step-by-step instructions

- Start by outlining why giving good feedback is important and by connecting the principles of good feedback to what technology is available, highlighting possible improvements in timeliness and student progress, as well as potential reductions in teacher workload. *(3–5 minutes)*

- If the technology allows, demonstrate alternative ways to give feedback. For example, you could record a quick audio message giving feedback to a particular student or to the class. Focus on how long that takes versus how long it would have taken to write it instead. Then highlight that students would get that important feedback immediately, not during the next lesson. Otherwise focus on the timeliness: feedback given and received in a more timely manner can have a positive impact on progress, as future lessons can be planned taking into account student work that has already been reviewed and feedback that has already been given. *(10–12 minutes)*
- Provide participants with a takeaway set of examples, illustrating various ways of providing feedback to individual students and to whole classes through technological means and highlighting the benefits discussed in the session.

Potential concern from teachers

I prefer face-to-face or one-to-one feedback.

Whenever a new technology is introduced, teachers often assume that they will be required to use it instead of other methods, not in addition to them. The introduction of technology does not herald the end of face-to-face feedback; it simply affords a greater range of options for teachers and students. Although face-to-face interaction is often preferable, it is not always possible, and that's when technology comes in.

15-minute session 4: Collaborating using office tools

Introduction to training

By collaboration I don't just mean student–student collaboration, such as pair- or group-work, but rather the ability for different people and teams of people to work together and simultaneously on one project. Here collaboration means student–student, but also student–teacher and teacher–teacher.

Cloud-based office tools such as Google for Education or Microsoft Office 365 now make it easier than ever to have multiple contributors to a document (e.g. an essay submitted by a student or a draft departmental policy), a spreadsheet (e.g. exam results or data gathered after an experiment) or a presentation (e.g. a set of slides submitted by a student or a lesson outline to be used by the department). The focus of this session ought to be on illustrating possible, new and more efficient workflows.

Preparation and resources required

- Practise sharing documents with your classes and with colleagues. Experiment with the sharing options (e.g. view only, view and edit, creating a URL link, etc.) so that you are, and will appear, comfortable with and knowledgeable about the functionality on the day.
- Book a suitable venue for the session. If staff all have their own devices, you could use a large open space with good wifi coverage; otherwise organise training in smaller groups and book a computer suite so that participants can use a computer. Projection facilities are desirable, but not essential.
- Create a document in advance of the session and be ready to share it with participants at the beginning of the session.
- Have at hand a series of examples of documents shared between different groups of people and explain clearly the steps from creation of the document, to sharing, to editing, to outcome. For example, you may wish to show an assignment that a student has shared with you, complete with your corrections and annotations.
- Prepare a quick guide outlining the main benefits of cloud-enabled collaboration and how to share and edit documents online.

Step-by-step instructions

- Start by outlining the benefits of online collaboration, such as expediency, timeliness, paperlessness and ubiquitous availability. Link these advantages to potential pedagogical benefits, such as improved teacher–student cooperation and timely feedback. *(4–5 minutes)*
- Share a document you prepared earlier with participants. For example, you could start a list by naming your favourite song and asking participants to do the same. This will illustrate how a group of people can work simultaneously on one document. *(4–5 minutes)*
- Then share a document that was created using this method. Describe how the document was created, shared and edited by two or more people, e.g. an essay featuring student work and teacher corrections or a group project completed by two or more students working together. *(5–6 minutes)*
- Provide participants with a link to a shared document outlining the benefits of online collaboration, basic how-to instructions and where to find further help.

Potential concern from teachers

I prefer marking on paper. I find marking on a screen very fiddly.

Online collaboration should be just another option, an extra tool in the teacher toolkit. As leaders in technology, we should actively avoid creating the impression that all work submitted needs to be looked at or marked using technology. That is plainly ludicrous, but it is an impression many teachers walk away with when they attend this kind of training. Rather, we should provide illustrations that allow teachers to visualise when this kind of collaboration may be more desirable. For example, coursework can be checked much more efficiently by teachers if they can simply open the same document a pupil is working on at any time during its completion, and sixth form tutors can supervise UCAS personal statements without exchanging multiple drafts.

15-minute session 5: Online quizzes

Introduction to training

Using online quizzing tools for whole-class participation is particularly effective if students have access to their own mobile device or the lesson is taking place in a computer suite. But it can still be used in ordinary classrooms with internet connection and projection facilities if you, for example, divide the class into two or three teams or allow the students to use their own smartphones. The session ought to focus on the benefits that the retrieval practice needed for quizzes can bring to learning, rather than on learning how to use the tool.

For quizzes to be beneficial to learning, they need to be relevant to the topic being covered, frequent (once or twice every lesson – ideal for starter and/or plenary activities) and low stakes. In fact, you should consider awarding house points or merits for knowing the answers instead of sanctions for not knowing.

Preparation and resources required

- Pick your favourite online quizzing tool and learn how to use it. At the time of writing, www.getkahoot.com and www.quizlet.com are two of the best such tools.
- Pick a topic and prepare a multiple choice quiz. Be specific and keep to a particular area of study. Avoid answers that are clearly wrong, as this would defeat the point of causing students to retrieve knowledge. Focus instead on answers that are plausible or that will generate a teachable moment when going over the answers.
- Book a suitable space for the training to take place. Taking the quizzes on mobile devices will be preferable, but a computer room can be used if that option is not available. Projection facilities to show the questions and scores are a must; speakers to play the tense gameshow music are optional.
- Prepare a short summary of the session's content, highlighting the benefits to the long-term retention of knowledge afforded by frequent retrieval practice and listing several online quizzing tools for teachers to try out and experiment with.

Step-by-step instructions

- Start by dispelling the notion that online quizzes are just a gimmick or a non-consequential game. As ever, focus on pedagogy: frequent, well-crafted quizzes have been shown to raise attainment significantly. This may be a game, but it is a serious one. *(2–3 minutes)*
- Challenge participants to take the quiz you have prepared for the occasion. Generate a little competition by offering a prize for the winner. Pause after each question to recap answers: Why was *x* the correct answer? Why was *y* the wrong answer? *(5–6 minutes)*
- Encourage participants to create a short quiz of their own, based on a topic area they are currently covering with one of their classes, and using the tool you have just demonstrated. *(5–6 minutes)*
- Hand out or email a pithy summary of the session with useful links to online tools and plenty of encouragement for colleagues. Consider doing it in the form of an online quiz.

Potential concern from teachers

This is just edutainment. I'd much rather be getting on with more serious stuff.

Potentially a very valid concern. I have seen teachers use quizzes as a reward at the end of the lesson, frequently using quizzes that are not even tangentially connected to the topic they have covered in the lesson. This makes no sense and is not pedagogically sound. However, if quizzes are well-crafted and meet the needs of the students for whom they have been carefully designed, then frequent retrieval practice opportunities provide students with opportunities for a more secure retention of knowledge and potentially a fast track to higher achievement in the subject.

Twilight session 1: An introduction to using technology in the classroom

Introduction to training

By now it should be apparent to you, the reader, that I believe technology trainers often focus on the technology, rather than on the pedagogy. This risks us falling into the rabbit hole of ever-changing technology and forgetting that using technology in the classroom should have one simple aim: to support and enhance the processes involved in teaching and learning. Everything else is secondary to this and you should prioritise accordingly.

This first twilight session is an opportunity for you and any colleagues supporting you to set out your stalls, not as happy-clappy evangelists of the new, but as teachers who are well-versed and confident in your subject content knowledge (you know what you teach), your pedagogical content knowledge (you know how you teach it) and your technological content knowledge (you are discerning and can pick the best tool for the job).

Planning document

Focus	Notes
Facilitators	• Remember you are not alone. Don't be afraid to take a leading role but do enlist the help of student Digital Leaders, staff Digital Champions or other colleagues who can demonstrate or illustrate the main points. • Consider making the main thrust of your session available to colleagues in advance, so that the session itself can be flipped, allowing it to transition more easily from a lecture to a more participatory, less formal TeachMeet style.
Topics covered	1. Exploration of the link between effective use of technology and great teaching. 2. Make explicit connections between what we know about effective teaching and how technology can support, deepen or accelerate those processes.
Preparation tasks	• Prepare a set of slides to illustrate how technology and pedagogy intersect. If possible and available, use photographs taken in your own context. • Prepare a further set of slides to use as conversation starters, featuring choice quotes from the literature you have read alongside this book. • Select a venue with good acoustics and projection facilities in good working order (nothing worse than a faint projector!). • Consider a seating plan. For example, you may want to sit departments together. • Have your IT support team check, double check and triple check that any technology you have planned to use works as required. • Prepare an online survey to gather feedback from participants after the session.

Focus	Notes
Resources required	• A well-crafted PowerPoint presentation which avoids overcrowding the slides with text and focuses instead on illustrating your points visually. • Projection facilities and audio equipment. • Presentation resources and handouts to be made available digitally. • A feedback online survey for participants.
Preparation time	**Beforehand:** • One to two hours putting together the PowerPoint and familiarising yourself with its content, topics to be covered and chosen quotes. **On the day:** • 15 minutes setting up the venue and double checking everything works as required.
Potential problems and solutions	**Problem:** Some colleagues may feel that technology has no place in their classroom and that they are fine as they are. **Solution:** Avoid prescribing technology as the solution to a perceived lack of 21st-century approaches and focus instead on linking effective technology with effective teaching. We all know excellent teachers, but all teachers can get better at teaching.
Possible follow-up tasks	During this session, offer to help teachers one to one or in small groups (e.g. departments) with the best possible use of technology in their subject areas. After the session, remind colleagues periodically of your offer and meet with colleagues.
Pass it on	Try to engender a culture of practice-sharing when it comes to technology, not one of accountability. Invite people to observe you in lessons and offer reciprocal informal observations that can be used to further inform your digital strategy and fine-tune your CPD programme.

Breakdown of session

Focus	Timing	Format	Content
Introduction: Why technology?	5–10 minutes	Presentation	Explain how technology alone is unlikely to improve teaching and learning. Use the TPACK model to illustrate this (www.TPACK.org).
What do we know about effective teaching?	10–15 minutes	Presentation and discussion	Spark discussion and reflection using choice quotes from *Make It Stick: The Science of Successful Learning*.
How can technology help?	10–15 minutes	Presentation	Give colleagues specific examples of how technology can contribute to improved teaching and learning.
Plenary	10–15 minutes	Group discussion	Possibly in subject-related groups, ask colleagues to reflect on what they have learnt today and how it could be applied in the teaching of their subjects.

Twilight session 2: Improving classroom instruction using the principles of dual coding

Introduction to training

This training session, like most other sessions in this series, should deal with technology implicitly while focusing on pedagogy explicitly. On this occasion, we will focus on the principle of dual coding and how knowledge of this, combined with technological knowledge, can have a positive impact on classroom instruction, learning and attainment.

Look through your department's bank of PowerPoint presentations or interactive whiteboard flipcharts and you'll find slides illustrated with content that is either relevant or completely superfluous and even distracting. Is that smiley emoji really required? Does that fancy animation add anything to the learning? While I accept that some illustrations may contribute to generating a positive learning environment, I suggest that our efforts are best directed at including illustrations that directly contribute to the learning. This is what cognitive psychologists call the dual-coding effect, which suggests that students learn more successfully when using a combination of words and images than when using just words or images on their own. This session will aim to make teachers aware of this explicitly so that they can bring this knowledge to bear when planning classroom-based instruction.

Planning document

Focus	Notes
Facilitators	• Consider whose lessons you have observed that already incorporate many of the principles behind dual coding.
	• Ask your colleagues to read this blog post in advance of the session: https://3starlearningexperiences.wordpress.com/2017/05/30/double-barrelled-learning-for-young-old/
Topics covered	1. Introduction of dual coding as a cognitive principle.
	2. Linking dual coding to everyday classroom technology, such as PowerPoint or interactive whiteboard software. This will be context-dependent.
	3. Discussion and sharing of possible strategies for adoption.
	4. Relevance of dual coding for students engaged in revision.

Focus	Notes
Preparation tasks	• Prepare a set of slides outlining the principles of dual coding and illustrating how they apply to the technology available in your setting. • Prepare a further set of slides to use as conversation starters, featuring quotes from the article highlighted above. • Select a venue with good projection facilities. • Consider a seating plan. For example, you may want to sit departments together to better enable discussion. • Prepare an online survey to gather feedback from participants after the session.
Resources required	• A well-crafted PowerPoint presentation that avoids overcrowding the slides with text and focuses instead on illustrating your points according to the principle of dual coding. • Projection facilities and audio equipment. • Presentation resources and handouts to be made available digitally. • A feedback online survey for participants.
Preparation time	**Beforehand:** • One to two hours putting together the PowerPoint and familiarising yourself with its content, topics to be covered and chosen quotes. **On the day:** • 15 minutes setting up the venue and double checking everything works as required.
Potential problems and solutions	**Problem:** Some colleagues may feel that they already 'do' dual coding and therefore the session has little relevance. **Solution:** Contrast examples of optimal use of dual coding with irrelevant use of illustrations. Use the ideas from the article provided. Highlight the importance of both teachers and students being aware of dual coding as a cognitive principle, so that the former can improve classroom instruction and the latter can enhance their revision and studying techniques.
Possible follow-up tasks	During this session, offer yourself to help teachers one to one or in small groups (e.g. departments) with the best possible use of technology in their subject areas. After the session, remind colleagues periodically of your offer and meet with colleagues.
Pass it on	Encourage colleagues to produce and share a PowerPoint or an interactive whiteboard flipchart that they have created following the session and save them in a shared folder so that everyone can access them.

Breakdown of session

Focus	Timing	Format	Content
Introduction: What is dual coding?	5–10 minutes	Presentation	Explain how dual coding can contribute to better learning. Illustrate with a picture from the blog link provided.
Examples of dual coding	10–15 minutes	Presentation and discussion	Spark discussion and reflection using further examples of dual coding in the school context. Try to illustrate this with examples from textbooks and existing subject-based PowerPoints or interactive whiteboard flipcharts.
How can technology help?	10–15 minutes	Presentation	Link dual coding explicitly to the functionality within PowerPoint and/ or interactive whiteboard flipcharts. For example, demonstrate how to create basic diagrams that help conceptualisation.
Plenary	10–15 minutes	Group discussion	Possibly in subject-related groups, ask colleagues to reflect on what they have learnt today and how it could be applied in the teaching of their subjects.

Twilight session 3: Exploring the principles of interleaving topics and spacing study

Introduction to training

Once again we refer to general teaching principles and link them to the technology that is available, in order to encourage a more discerning application. On this occasion we will focus on interleaving, which is the principle of switching ideas during a study session or, indeed, a lesson or sequence of lessons. Applying the principle of interleaving forces students to go back over ideas. This has been shown to strengthen understanding, as students make progress by making links between the different ideas they are being exposed to.

Spacing study, which is the practice of revising topics by chunking revision over a period of time instead of massing study into a final mammoth revision session, say, before an examination, is closely linked to interleaving. Both principles are relevant to teachers because they can be applied when planning lessons and sequences of lessons, as well as when resources are being made available for later access, for example in a virtual learning environment or digital content management system.

Planning document

Focus	Notes
Facilitators	• Liaise closely with your Deputy Head Academic or Director of Studies to explore how your session dovetails with the school's wider learning strategy. They may be able to suggest colleagues with the requisite pedagogical knowledge and help you with this session. • Ask your colleagues to access, download and explore the resources on interleaving and spacing available here: https://teachinghow2s.com/cogsci/learner-materials
Topics covered	1. Introduction of the concepts of interleaving and spacing study. 2. Sample lesson plans briefly illustrating interleaving in action. 3. Sample schemes of work highlighting possible spacing of topics. 4. Explicit linking of interleaving to presentation and interactive whiteboard software and spacing to virtual learning environments or content management systems.
Preparation tasks	• Prepare a set of slides defining interleaving and spacing. • Prepare a sample lesson plan and a sample scheme of work or programme of study illustrating the application of these concepts. • Select a venue with good projection facilities. • Consider a seating plan. For example, you may want to sit departments together to better enable discussion. • Prepare an online survey to gather feedback from participants after the session.
Resources required	• A PowerPoint presentation containing relevant definitions, samples and illustrations. • Projection facilities and audio equipment. • Presentation resources and handouts to be made available digitally. • A feedback online survey for participants.
Preparation time	**Beforehand:** • One to two hours reading up on the concepts of interleaving and spacing, preparing a PowerPoint and familiarising yourself with its content. **On the day:** • 15 minutes setting up the venue and double checking everything works as required.
Potential problems and solutions	**Problem:** Teachers may feel that interleaving and spacing feel less effective, citing that students prefer it when they spend longer on one single topic. **Solution:** Students may well prefer to dedicate longer periods to one topic rather than interleave topics. This is because interleaving is more effortful and thus more tasking. It is precisely because students are made to think harder about a topic that they can make links, improve their understanding and make faster progress. It is counter-intuitive, but there is a significant body of research backing these principles.

Focus	Notes
Possible follow-up tasks	During this session, offer yourself to help teachers one to one or in small groups (e.g. departments) with the best possible use of technology in their subject areas. After the session, remind colleagues periodically of your offer and meet with colleagues and follow up any queries or concerns.
Pass it on	Encourage colleagues to produce a sample plan for a lesson or sequence of lessons. Heads of department or subject leaders could be asked to adapt their schemes of work or programmes of study to take these concepts into account. Sharing these plans and schemes of work digitally in a central bank would become a valuable resource for reference.

Breakdown of session

Focus	Timing	Format	Content
Introduction: What are interleaving and spacing?	5–10 minutes	Presentation	Use the PDF documents available from the links provided to illustrate the concepts of interleaving and spacing.
Planning a lesson with interleaving in mind	10–15 minutes	Presentation	Provide one or two lesson plans that illustrate how we can make the most of the principle of interleaving in a lesson.
Planning schemes of work with spacing in mind	10–15 minutes	Presentation and discussion	Provide a sample scheme of work that incorporates the principle of spacing and contrast it with one that doesn't. Use them to kick off discussion and debate.
Plenary: Where does the technology come in?	10–15 minutes	Presentation followed by group discussion	Make explicit links between the principles and technology such as interactive whiteboard flipcharts and virtual learning environments. Focus on how they can contribute to these principles.

Twilight session 4: Encouraging learners to plan, monitor and evaluate their own learning

Introduction to training

Metacognition and self-regulation strategies are hugely beneficial for students and have been linked to huge improvements in attainment. However, they are difficult to implement effectively, as they require 'buy-in' from every section of the school, not least the students! In other words, this cannot be one person's pet project, but rather integral to the school's strategy to improve teaching and learning.

By teaching students practical strategies to plan, monitor and evaluate their own learning, this approach allows them to develop an awareness about how they learn best. But learning can be facilitated by a variety of tools, including digital resources. It is in this context that self-regulation acquires a new dimension: not only are students' needs better served by learning to plan, monitor and self-evaluate, but also by learning to self-regulate the use of the different tools and resources available to them.

Planning document

Focus	Notes
Facilitators	• You may want to enlist the help of your learning support team and the person or team in charge of PSHE, as you seek to promote good study skills and learning habits, and then link them to the appropriate use of technology. • Ask your colleagues to read and explore the resources on metacognition available here: https://educationendowmentfoundation.org.uk/resources/teaching-learning-toolkit/meta-cognition-and-self-regulation/
Topics covered	1. Introduction of the concepts of metacognition and self-regulation. 2. Outlining sample strategies that foster metacognition (see chapter 4). 3. Discussion: What does this mean in this context? 4. Linking self-regulation explicitly to the appropriate use of technology.
Preparation tasks	• Prepare a set of slides defining the concepts of metacognition and self-regulation. Use the resources in the link provided, above, to help you. • Prepare an additional set of slides outlining possible metacognitive strategies, as discussed in chapter 4. • Select a venue with good acoustics and projection facilities. • Consider a seating plan. For example, you may want to sit departments together to better enable discussion. • Prepare an online survey to gather feedback from participants after the session.
Resources required	• A PowerPoint presentation containing relevant definitions, samples and illustrations. • Projection facilities and audio equipment. • Presentation resources and handouts to be made available digitally. • A feedback online survey for participants.
Preparation time	**Beforehand:** • One to two hours familiarising yourself with the concepts of metacognition and self-regulation and preparing a PowerPoint. Aim to incorporate into your presentation other principles covered thus far, such as dual coding and interleaving. **On the day:** • 15 minutes setting up the venue and double checking everything works as required.

Focus	Notes
Potential problems and solutions	**Problem:** Students may feel that these strategies require too much effort. Teachers may feel students are better served by spoon-feeding them what they need to know. **Solution:** Students are right. These strategies are more effortful, as they require a growing degree of independence and responsibility for their own learning. This is why they are successful. Explain clearly to students and teachers the reasoning behind the strategies, instead of simply expecting them to apply them. Get this right and a virtuous circle of improving attainment is generated.
Possible follow-up tasks	During this session, offer yourself to help teachers one to one or in small groups (e.g. departments) with the best possible use of technology in their subject areas. After the session, remind colleagues periodically of your offer and meet with colleagues and follow up any queries or concerns.
Pass it on	Encourage colleagues to develop subject- or topic-specific metacognitive strategies along the lines of those outlined in chapter 4. Share these examples digitally in a central resource bank.

Breakdown of session

Focus	Timing	Format	Content
Introduction: What are metacognition and regulation?	5–10 minutes	Presentation	Use the PDF documents available from the links provided to define the concepts of metacognition and self-regulation.
Explore different metacognition strategies	10–15 minutes	Presentation and discussion	Provide examples of metacognitive strategies in at least two different, contrasting subjects, e.g. English and Maths.
Where does the technology come in?	10–15 minutes	Presentation	Make explicit links between the principles of metacognition/self-regulation and the available technology, e.g. using visualisers or PowerPoints to present students with increasing challenging material or using digital learning spaces to provide students with the means to access content and self-evaluate on demand.
Plenary	10–15 minutes	Group discussion	If possible, group participants according to subject specialism and ask them to reflect on how what they have learnt today can be applied in their subject.

Twilight session 5: The secret powers of testing

Introduction to training

Traditionally, tests have almost solely been used as summative assessments, checking how much students have learnt at the end of a unit of study. So we have end of unit tests, end of term tests and end of year exams. Clearly, benchmarking student progress is important, but tests have an ace hidden up their sleeves: they are very good at helping us learn, not because we usually revise beforehand – though, clearly, that is a factor – but because they force us to retrieve knowledge from memory. It follows then that more tests may be more beneficial to the learning than to the assessing, and, therefore, more tests may be not just desirable, but actually a booster for higher attainment.

Proposing more testing may not make you more popular among teachers (who will assume more marking) or students (who will assume more pressure). It is important therefore to lower the stakes of these more frequent interim tests so that students do not feel extra pressure and instead feel the benefits of improved learning. In the modern school context, low-stakes tests can be prepared digitally in a variety of ways. Both Google for Education and Microsoft Office 365 offer survey creation tools that can turn into tests at the flick of a switch (this means no marking!), and online quizzing tools, such as those proposed earlier in this chapter in *15-minute session 5*, can turn a test into an enjoyable classroom activity.

Planning document

Focus	Notes
Facilitators	• Consider inviting colleagues who already test students frequently to share their experiences in this session.
	• Ask your colleagues to read this article about how different teachers apply the principles of frequent retrieval practice in their lessons: http://www.learningscientists.org/blog/2016/6/5/weekly-digest-13?rq=retrieval%20practice
Topics covered	1. Introduction of the concept of retrieval practice and its benefits to learning.
	2. Watch this three-minute video outlining retrieval practice strategies: https://www.youtube.com/watch?v=Pjrqc6UMDKM
	3. Discussion: What does this mean in this context?
	4. Linking retrieval practice explicitly to the technology available in your context.

Focus	Notes
Preparation tasks	• Prepare a set of slides outlining the benefits of retrieval practice. Use the resources and videos in the links provided, above. • Prepare an additional set of slides outlining possible retrieval practice opportunities, as afforded by digital flashcards, online tests and quizzes. This is context-dependent – for example, your virtual learning environment may feature quizzing or testing functionality. • Select a venue with good acoustics and projection facilities. • Consider a seating plan. For example, you may want to sit departments together to better enable discussion. • Prepare an online survey to gather feedback from participants after the session.
Resources required	• A PowerPoint presentation containing relevant definitions, samples and illustrations. • Projection facilities and audio equipment. • Presentation resources and handouts to be made available digitally. • A feedback online survey for participants.
Preparation time	***Beforehand:*** • One to two hours reading about retrieval practice and preparing a well-designed PowerPoint. Aim to incorporate all the cognitive principles studies thus far. ***On the day:*** • 15 minutes setting up the venue and double checking everything works as required.
Potential problems and solutions	***Problem:*** Teachers may feel that more frequent testing takes up lesson time and adds to marking. ***Solution:*** Online tests are often self-marking and, when they are not, you may want to get students to mark each other's tests, contributing to their metacognitive and self-regulating skills. In addition, these tests can be done for homework, say once every fortnight. This will have a positive impact both on learning and on an improved teacher workload, as this generates either no marking or considerably less marking.
Possible follow-up tasks	During this session, offer yourself to help teachers one to one or in small groups (e.g. departments) with the best possible use of technology in their subject areas. After the session, remind colleagues periodically of your offer and meet with colleagues and follow up any queries or concerns.
Pass it on	Encourage colleagues to devise a multiple choice test for a topic using Google for Education or Microsoft Office 365. It may be that your virtual learning environment or content management system is another option.

Breakdown of session

Focus	Timing	Format	Content
Introduction: Why frequent retrieval practice?	5–10 minutes	Presentation	Using the link provided above, show the video introducing the concept of retrieval practice. Emphasise how retrieval practice can be low-stakes or no-stakes.
What does retrieval practice mean in practice?	10–15 minutes	Presentation	Provide further examples of retrieval practice, ideally using existing resources that do not necessarily rely on technology, e.g. teacher questioning, quizzes, tests and flashcards.
Where does the technology come in?	10–15 minutes	Presentation and discussion	Make explicit links between the principles explored in this session and the technology that can help you deliver frequent low-stakes tests, e.g. your virtual learning environment, office tools such as Office 365 and Google, and online quiz makers such as Quizlet and Kahoot.
Plenary	10–15 minutes	Group discussion	In subject-related groups, encourage colleagues to discuss how retrieval practice can help their students, and how technology can support learning in this context.

3 Evaluation and next steps

This final chapter encourages you to assess the impact of both your technology implementation and the training sessions across the school, with the aim of evaluating their success and identifying what steps might be required next. By now, you probably understand that technology implementations cannot be pursued without bringing in wider teaching and learning considerations. If pet or vanity projects ever get off the ground, they are often doomed to failure in the medium to long term. Therefore, making your implementation integral to the wider school development plan and bringing in colleagues from across the different sections of the school on board from the outset is essential.

For this reason, your evaluation needs to begin at the outset and not at an arbitrarily chosen end point (with successful technology implementations, there is no visible end point) and continue, ideally indefinitely, so that it formatively assesses your implementation and training as it develops.

Evaluating the success of the CPD sessions

Evaluation can take a variety of guises, but asking your colleagues to return qualitative data in the form of answers to a questionnaire is probably the most illuminating way to identify the successes and failures of the CPD you have organised. A crucial guiding principle is to aim to obtain maximum granularity (what is working well or not, for whom and why) while preserving anonymity. Using an online survey or questionnaire sends a powerful message to colleagues that you are serious about the use of technology and provides an example of effective use of technology for a purpose. Below is a sample questionnaire that you can use or adapt according to the needs of your own setting:

About you

Q1 – What is your role in school?

Drop down/multiple choice

teacher – teaching assistant – head of department – head of year – senior leadership

Q2 – What is your subject family?

Drop down/multiple choice

maths and sciences – arts and humanities – other

About the training

Q3 – The aims and objectives of the training were clear

Agree/disagree with statement

1= disagree completely, 2= agree a little, 3= mostly agree, 4= agree, 5= strongly agree

Q4 – The training was relevant to my role

Agree/disagree with statement

1= disagree completely, 2= agree a little, 3= mostly agree, 4= agree, 5= strongly agree

Q5 – The trainer was knowledgeable

Agree/disagree with statement

1= disagree completely, 2= agree a little, 3= mostly agree, 4= agree, 5= strongly agree

Q6 – I was able to ask questions and seek clarification

Agree/disagree with statement

1= disagree completely, 2= agree a little, 3= mostly agree, 4= agree, 5= strongly agree

Q7 – The training helped me understand how technology can support teaching and learning

Agree/disagree with statement

1= disagree completely, 2= agree a little, 3= mostly agree, 4= agree, 5= strongly agree

Q8 – The training was well-organised and effective

Agree/disagree with statement

1= disagree completely, 2= agree a little, 3= mostly agree, 4= agree, 5= strongly agree

Q9 – I would recommend this training to a colleague

Agree/disagree with statement

1= disagree completely, 2= agree a little, 3= mostly agree, 4= agree, 5= strongly agree

Your feedback

Q10 – What did you learn today that will be most valuable to you and why?

Q11 – What did you learn today that will be least valuable to you and why?

Q12 – How has today's session developed your understanding of using technology for learning?

Q13 – What can you commit to trying as a result of this training?

Q14 – What did you learn today that will inform or change your teaching practice?

Q15 – Do you have any other comments?

```

```

It may be tempting to want to collect this information immediately after the training, and there may be good reasons for this: expediency, catch them while you can, etc. However, I have found it pays to allow colleagues time for reflection and the opportunity to answer the questionnaire in their own time when they are not in a rush to go home or to the next lesson. The fact that the questionnaire can be emailed to your colleagues and they can complete it online ought to facilitate this.

Avoid hoarding the information. Share it with colleagues, your line manager and even members of SLT. Actively seek their advice and suggestions for improvement. Even though the final decision about how to move the training forward may be yours alone, the more suggestions you receive, the more options for improvement you'll have at your disposal.

Evaluating the success of the technology implementation

The success of the CPD sessions is inextricably intertwined with the success of the technology implementation that you set out to achieve. Evaluating the former will contribute to the evaluation of the latter, and vice versa. In this section, we will suggest types of evidence and questions that can be asked to try to evaluate how well technology is being adopted in the classroom. These questions are not meant to be asked after a training session, as they are not dependent on specific events, but rather they seek to ascertain to what extent the combination of training and new technology is contributing to more effective use of technology to support teaching and learning.

Lesson observations

Observing colleagues in their lessons will give you a very accurate picture of whether technology is being adopted to support teaching and learning. If you are a line manager or member of SLT, frequent lesson observations may well be a part of your role. But if you are not, you will need to find alternative ways to observe lessons. Asking people to invite you is one very good option, but bear in mind this is likely to offer a skewed perspective, as it is those who are using technology more or more effectively who are more likely to have the confidence to invite you to their lessons.

Lesson observations are potentially stressful experiences for those being observed. Please emphasise incessantly that the purpose of your observation is to see how your implementation is developing, not to pass judgement on your colleagues' teaching. Above all, avoid grading lessons in any way, shape or form. Just watch and learn.

Lesson study

Lesson study can be defined as lesson observation plus. You can either work with a group of staff Digital Champions, with another working party or you can work in a smaller group of three to four teachers to collaborate with one another and discuss explicitly how best the technology can be applied in the classroom. In a lesson study, colleagues plan an actual lesson and then observe how their ideas work in real life in front of students. Participants then meet again to discuss and reflect on what they have observed, in turn informing planning of the next lesson in the lesson study.

Learning walks

The term learning walks has become a euphemism for stricter performance management and increased accountability in many settings. I would like to take you back to the original, truer spirit of the learning walks idea, which is to contribute to a collegiate, open-door environment in which teachers freely share and discuss their practice. Applied in this spirit, learning walks can become your most accurate tool to evaluate the extent of the success of your implementation and the accompanying training, as you visit lessons freely and get glimpses of what teachers are teaching, how they are teaching and, if you include students in your evaluation, how they feel about the effectiveness of the implementation.

Questionnaires

Multiple choice and short answer questions are great for obtaining feedback after a training session. These questionnaires should be short, sharp and not onerous to those answering. However, sometimes it is better to delve a little deeper into the views and feeling of your colleagues by asking questions that are a little more probing and thought-provoking. Below is a template with suggested questions; please feel free to use it verbatim but I would strongly suggest that you tailor it to your setting:

Evaluating the technology implementation	
In answering these questions, consider what you have learnt in our training sessions, to what extent you have been able to put it into practice and its success or failure.	
How do your views about what makes great teaching and the use of technology align?	
Do you think the culture (what we do) and the climate (how what we do feels) in the school support or hinder the technology implementation?	
What opportunities have there been in your department to explore the application of technology for learning?	
Have the schemes of work in your department changed as a result of the introduction of technology?	
How has your attitude changed regarding the use of technology in the classroom?	
How have your students' attitudes changed regarding the use of technology in the classroom?	
What changes do you need to make to help you embed the use of technology in your lessons?	
Is the use of technology contributing to or hindering the learning that goes on in your classroom? Why?	
What would you say is working really well for you?	
What would you say is not working well at all for you?	
Have you identified any improvement in outcomes that can be linked directly or indirectly to the introduction of technology?	
Have you identified any deterioration in outcomes that can be linked directly or indirectly to the introduction of technology?	
Is there anything else you would like to add?	

Clearly, questionnaires such as this are more onerous for your colleagues but they can yield a huge amount of valuable information to help you steer your training and the focus of your implementation. They too can be completed online. Please bear in mind your colleagues are busy folk, so you should be careful to not overburden them with unnecessary extra work. You would be well advised to avoid certain pinch points in the year, such as immediately after school assessments or internal exams and around report deadlines.

Interviews

Face-to-face interviews can be a fantastic way to get to the bottom of issues raised in training sessions and questionnaires. Sometimes the best way to deal with the concerned or sceptical colleague is to see them face to face to discuss in more detail the reasons why something is or isn't working, giving you the opportunity to address the concerns or reasons for scepticism in a private, sympathetic atmosphere. Sort out these concerns for them and you can potentially gain your strongest allies.

But interviews are also a wonderful opportunity to get around and be visible, putting a face (yours) to the technology implementation and contributing to reinforce the message that technology is just another tool and that you are on their side.

Becoming a beacon of best practice

In recent years, there has been a greater call for teachers and schools to use research evidence to inform their interventions and implementations. This is a welcome development, as it provides us with sign posts that can lead to better-informed and improved practice. But we must always keep in mind that research findings tell you what was, not what will be. When it comes to using technology in the classroom, the research body is surprisingly thin. One of the reasons for this is that there is not a clear definition of what using technology in the classroom actually means: is it using computer programmes to teach students certain topics? Is it learning programming or learning to code? Is it using interactive whiteboards or visualisers? Or is it using mobile devices? And, if so, for what?

This is the reason why this book has focused on studying what we know about great teaching and learning and has sought to develop a conceptual Venn diagram in which great pedagogy and technology intersect to highlight how their thoughtful, discerning combination can result in improved outcomes for students.

When it comes to evaluating the success of your implementations, you will not need to show evidence of how technology or your training would work elsewhere; you just need to show how technology has been successful in your context. If the staffroom is buzzing with discussions about how the technology helps with teaching, if colleagues are signing up to lead training sessions on your behalf, if students and parents feel their learning is supported using technology, and if improved outcomes can reasonably be linked directly or indirectly to the technology, the chances are that your approach has been a success and your school is well on its way to becoming a beacon of best practice.

Bibliography and further reading

3-Star Learning Experiences (2017), 'Double-barrelled learning for young & old'. Available at: https://3starlearningexperiences.wordpress.com/2017/05/30/double-barrelled-learning-for-young-old/ [Accessed 13 Jun. 2017].

Brown, P., Roediger, H. and McDaniel, M. (2014). *Make It Stick:The Science of Successful Learning*. 1st ed. Cambridge, Massachusetts: The Belknap Press of Harvard University Press.

Buck, A. (2016). *Leadership Matters*. Woodbridge: John Catt Educational.

Carey, B. (2015). *How We Learn*. London: Pan Macmillan.

Coe, R., Aloisi, C., Higgins, S. and Major, L. E. (2014). 'What makes great teaching?' The Sutton Trust http://www.suttontrust.com/researcharchive/great-teaching/

Education Endowment Foundation, *Teaching and Learning Toolkit* [online] Available at: http://educationendowmentfoundation.org.uk/toolkit/ [Accessed 13 Jun. 2017].

Hattie, J. and Yates, G. (2014). *Visible Learning and the Science of How We Learn*. 1st ed. London: Routledge.

Higgins, S., Xiao, Z. and Katsipataki, M. (2012). 'The Impact of Digital Technology on Learning: A Summary for the Education Endowment Foundation'. [online] Available at: https://v1.educationendowmentfoundation.org.uk/uploads/pdf/The_Impact_of_Digital_Technologies_on_Learning_FULL_REPORT_(2012).pdf [Accessed 3 Aug. 2017].

Hughes, J. E. (2000). 'Teaching English with technology: Exploring teacher learning and practice', (doctoral dissertation), Michigan State University, East Lansing, MI. [online] Available at: http://techedges.org/wp-content/uploads/2015/11/Hughes_Full_Dissertation.pdf [Accessed 3 Aug. 2017].

Luckin, R., Bligh, B., Manches, A., Ainsworth, S., Crook, C. and Noss, R. (2012). 'Decoding learning: The proof, promise and potential of digital education'. [online] Available at: www.nesta.org.uk/library/documents/DecodingLearningReport_v12.pdf [Accessed 3 Aug. 2017]

Mishra, P. and Koehler, M. J. (2006). 'Technological pedagogical content knowledge: A framework for teacher knowledge'. *Teachers College Record*, 108, (6), 1017–1054. doi: 10.1111/j.1467-9620.2006.00684.x.

Norrish, D., Baker, M., Edwards, D., Picardo, J. and Webster, A. (2014). *Educate 1-to-1: The Secrets to Successfully Planning, Implementing and Sustaining Change through Mobile Learning in Schools.*

Puentedura, R. (2014). *Learning, Technology, and the SAMR Model: Goals, Processes, and Practice.* [online] Available at: http://www.hippasus.com/rrpweblog/archives/2014/06/29/LearningTechnologySAMRModel.pdf [Accessed 13 Jun. 2017].

Rosenshine, B., (2012). 'Principles of instruction: Research-based strategies that all teachers should know'. *American Educator.* [online] Available at: https://www.aft.org/sites/default/files/periodicals/Rosenshine.pdf [Accessed 13 Jun. 2017].

Teachinghow2s.com. *Cognitive Science Learner Materials – TeachingHOW2s.* [online] Available at: https://teachinghow2s.com/cogsci/learner-materials [Accessed 13 Jun. 2017].

The Learning Scientists. *Weekly Digest #13: How Teachers Implement Retrieval in their Classrooms.* [online] Available at: http://www.learningscientists.org/blog/2016/6/5/weekly-digest-13?rq=retrieval%20practice [Accessed 13 Jun. 2017].

Wiliam, D. and Leahy, S. (2015). *Embedding Formative Assessment.* 1st ed. West Palm Beach, Fla.: Learning Sciences.

Willingham, D. (2013). *Why Don't Students Like School?* Hoboken, N.J.: Wiley.

Index